The Disbelief Habit

Yong Kang Chan, best known as Nerdy Creator, is a blogger, mindfulness teacher, and private tutor. Having low self-esteem growing up, he has read a lot of books on personal growth, psychology, and spirituality.

Based in Singapore, Yong Kang teaches mathematics and accounting to his students. On his website, he writes blog posts on self-compassion and mindfulness to help introverts and people with low self-esteem.

Please visit his website at www.nerdycreator.com.

The Disbelief Habit

How to Use Doubt to Make Peace with Your Inner Critic

YONG KANG CHAN

RUPA

Published by
Rupa Publications India Pvt. Ltd 2022
7/16, Ansari Road, Daryaganj
New Delhi 110002

Sales centres:
Allahabad Bengaluru Chennai
Hyderabad Jaipur Kathmandu
Kolkata Mumbai

P-ISBN: 978-93-5520-859-0
E-ISBN: 978-93-5520-860-6

First impression 2022

10 9 8 7 6 5 4 3 2 1

Printed in India

CONTENTS

Preface

If I had listened to the thoughts in my head two years ago, you would not be reading this book. Near the end of 2015, I was jobless and I experienced major depression.

During the two months before my depression, I was feeling ashamed of myself. My mind went into a downward spiral. Every day I had to deal with endless self-criticism and negative thoughts. I couldn't stop my mind from berating me and, worst of all, I believed everything it told me. I believed no one needed me. I believed that I would die if I didn't get another job soon. All this criticism seemed so true to me at the time. I couldn't control my tears; clearly, my emotions were out of control.

I had allowed my inner critic to tear me apart completely.

One day, I found myself at the river thinking: *Jump in and you'll end your suffering.* Just so you know, I didn't plan for suicide. I was feeling frustrated at home, so I went out for a walk to take a breather. The idea of jumping in was just one of those random thoughts that crossed my mind when I was at the river. Luckily for me, I didn't trust these thoughts and didn't act on them.

But from that day onward, I realized something important – I needed to be more mindful of my thoughts because they aren't always helpful or correct.

In fact, they are mostly wrong.

If you are interested in learning more about my experience with depression, please read my memoir, *The Emotional Gift*.

This new book, *The Disbelief Habit*, is about how we doubt our thoughts, especially the critical ones. I'm so grateful that I survived depression in 2015, and that I am able to pass this message on to you.

In my mid-twenties, I learned how to correct my negative thinking and be more positive. However, sometimes what I *think* is positive might not actually turn out to be positive or make me any happier. Occasionally, it creates more stress and frustration.

After I survived depression, I began to read more

books on spirituality and mindfulness, I learned to distance myself from my mind. Now, I don't trust my thoughts 100% anymore. I don't consider my thoughts to be absolute truth, but merely suggestions and opinions. Whether to believe and use these thoughts or not is really up to me.

As with my other books, the writing in this one is as simple as possible. Most of the insights are drawn from my own experiences and observations. If you are looking for something that has been scientifically researched, this book might not be suitable for you. But if you are someone who is open to self-exploration and learning through anecdotes, it will resonate with you.

My mission in life is to make the world a more peaceful place for all of us. This starts with helping individuals connect with their inner peace and become more self-compassionate. By reading this book, you are already a part of this movement. So thank you!

Yong Kang Chan

Singapore, 2017

Introduction

Stopping Your Negative Thoughts

"Peace cannot be kept by force; it can only be achieved by understanding."

— ALBERT EINSTEIN

Have you tried to stop the negative voice in your head? How successful have you been?

Like most people, when I was younger I tried many different exercises and techniques to release my negative thoughts. I also read various blog posts and books, watched numerous videos, and bought online programs to assist in my study of positivity. Generally, this worked, and I built a decent level of self-esteem and confidence. There were still times when I was hard on myself. However, I wasn't overly bothered because it wasn't as intense as my teenage years had been. So I simply corrected my negative self-beliefs and made them more positive, thinking that, eventually, my negative thoughts would go away. I thought it was up to me to fix my thinking.

It wasn't until years later, when I found myself jobless and in a downward spiral with depression, that I realized, "Hey, the critical voice is still there. It didn't go away. It was just lurking in the background, waiting for the opportunity to criticize and shame me. It can still turn my life upside down, and I don't think *it will ever go away.*"

Everyone has a critical voice in their heads. This is the voice that tells us:

- You will never amount to anything.
- You can't be wealthy.
- You are not beautiful enough.
- You are a bad parent.
- No one loves you.

The intensity and the things you are criticized for might be different. Some people might get agitated with themselves easily for dropping something on the floor. Others might punish themselves for not reaching their goals. We all have an inner voice that finds fault and judges us. It is commonly known as the "inner critic." It's a subpersonality that our minds have created to help us cope with certain situations and emotions.

Most of us think that silencing the inner critic is the solution to our problems, but it's not. Stopping the negative thoughts in our heads might help temporarily, but ultimately we need to learn how to deal with the critical voice. The inner critic has a purpose to fulfill. When your inner critic criticizes you, it might want you to do better, or perhaps it wants to protect you from making mistakes and harming yourself. You cannot stop it from doing its job.

Even though we might blame our inner critic for making us feel unworthy, it's not the only subpersonality that is responsible for our lack of self-worth.

Many People Living in the Same Head

You have probably noticed there is more than one voice in your head, and that each voice has a different opinion and tone. Some of them are harsh, like the inner critic. Others are mild and subdued. The mind subdivides itself into different parts in order to help us cope with various situations. Each subpersonality has a unique purpose and beliefs about what is good or bad for us. It's as though there are many people living inside the same head.

When we experience self-criticism, it's not just the working of the inner critic, but also the result of collaboration between the various subpersonalities. One part of the mind creates the problem and the other jumps in to fix it.

The inner critic doesn't work in isolation.

There is no need for criticism when all of our subpersonalities obey what the inner critic dictates. However, the other parts of the mind are never going to obey the inner critic because they have their own agendas. One part might just want to have fun and doesn't want to work at all. Another part might sacrifice too much in order to gain approval from others. There might be yet another part that engages us in impulsive behaviors or addictions in order to distract us from feeling the shame and hurt inflicted by the inner critic.

Stopping self-criticism only reduces the frequency of our pain and prevents the pain from surfacing. It doesn't resolve the underlying emotions that are buried deep down inside our minds and bodies. For the inner critic to be able to hurt us, there must be a part of the mind that wants to feel the shame and wallow in self-pity. When we are at our most vulnerable, we *unconsciously* identify ourselves with this subpersonality. We believe that we are the victim and the inner critic is the enemy that is constantly bombarding us with negative thoughts.

The truth is we are neither the victim nor the inner critic. As discussed in my book, *Empty Your Cup,* we are not the identities that our minds create. We are the awareness behind the voices. We observe the conflict between the different parts of our minds, and we have the ability to *choose* which subpersonality we want to listen to.

Two Layers of Suffering

There are two layers of suffering. One comes from the inner critic and the other comes from our unconscious reactions to self-criticism. I call the former, "The Mental Layer" and the latter, "The Reaction Layer."

Most of us try to stop our suffering by working on the Mental Layer and changing our beliefs in the subconscious mind. With proper tools and techniques, we can reduce our self-criticism significantly. However, changing our beliefs can also be tedious, complicated, and tricky.

First, it's not always easy to judge which beliefs are best. For example, we might think that getting more money and a better job will make us happier, but our assumptions might be wrong.

Second, our subconscious minds contain many beliefs, just like a computer has many different files and components. We are not sure how many beliefs our minds hold, and their relationships with one another, because we can't see them. We might think we have changed our negative beliefs, but they might not be really gone. Just like a computer; when you delete a file, it's not really deleted. You can still recover the file if you know how to do it. But you wouldn't want to change the files in the system if you don't have the expertise because it might affect the other files and crash your computer.

Third, each subpersonality has its own set of beliefs, so they are bound to have some disagreement. Most of our beliefs will continue to conflict with one another no matter how we change them.

Maybe self-criticism isn't the problem,
but rather how we react to the criticism that is the problem.

This book focuses on the second layer of suffering, the reaction layer. Most of our suffering comes from our reactions. When we try to fight the inner critic and prevent it from intruding into our minds, we create an internal war instead of inner peace. We also make ourselves feel worse when we dwell on the criticism. Our reaction determines how much *more* we will suffer.

In the book, *The Fifth Agreement,* Don Miguel Ruiz and Don Jose Ruiz wrote, "True justice is to pay one time for every mistake we make." If you break the law, you go to jail once. You don't go to jail several times for the same crime. When you do something wrong, let your inner critic tell you what is necessary *once,* and then move on with your life. You don't have to argue with it or make yourself suffer *more* by punishing yourself several times for the same thing.

We don't have control over the thoughts our subconscious minds create. They are random and conceived even when we are not thinking about anything. However, if we are able to accept this and focus on what we can control instead, then there will be no issue at all. We can't stop the inner critic from attacking us, but we don't have to be the victim and believe everything it tells us. We can *choose* how we react to self-criticism. Simply doing so can remove much of our suffering.

About This Book

This book is about building a habit of disbelief. Not everything our minds tell us is true, especially our negative self-talk and self-criticism.

In the first part of the book, we will learn about why disbelieving our thoughts can help reduce our suffering. In the first two chapters, we will explore how biased our thoughts are, and how self-criticism has become a habit. In the subsequent two chapters, we will learn to identify our current reactions to the inner critic and what disbelieving is – and isn't.

In the second part of the book, Chapters 5 to 9 are about learning how to doubt our thoughts and make disbelief a habit. Most of the suggestions in this book are what a mindfulness practitioner would do. Here, I've simply broken them down into steps and provided more details for each step.

At the end of this book, you will find a summary of these steps. I encourage you to use it as a reference and to also create your own steps. There is no right or wrong when it comes to self-compassion and mindfulness practice.

It's all about finding a routine that suits you.

In this book, I've used examples from my real life, and because I'm a tutor, I also share a lot of insights from my interaction with students and parents. Of course, I've changed the names of the people involved to protect their privacy.

Now, let's start by understanding why it's important to doubt our thoughts.

PART ONE

Why Disbelieve?

My mathematics student, Nelly, once asked me, "How can I stop making mistakes?" She understood most of the mathematics concepts. However, every time she got back her results, she told me she could have scored better *if* she wasn't careless.

During my lessons with her, I realized she *was* prone to making careless mistakes, but how could I stop her from making them? She had asked a great question and I didn't have an immediate response. I started wondering: *Why am I so careful? What did I do differently? What is my secret formula?*

It took awhile before I replied, "Practice and develop the habit of doubting your thoughts."

Chapter 1

Don’t Take Your Thoughts Too Seriously

“Believing yourself is one of the worst things you can do because you’ve been telling yourself lies your whole life.”

— DON MIGUEL RUIZ, THE FIFTH AGREEMENT

Is the dress white and gold or blue and black? This is the question that got the world debating in 2015.

It all started in Cheshire Oaks Mall, just north of Chester, United Kingdom, when Cecilia Bleasdale snapped a photo of the striped dress she intended to wear to her daughter’s wedding. She sent the photo to her daughter, Grace, who was living in Colonsay, Scotland, and asked her for her opinion on the blue and black dress. Grace was confused because she could only see a white and gold dress in the picture. "Mom, if you think the dress is blue and black, you need to go and see the doctor," she said.

After some discussion, Grace decided to show the photo to her fiancé, and they also disagreed on what the colors were. So the bride shared the image on Facebook with her friends to validate the colors. But instead of coming to a conclusion, the debate continued. Some people said the dress was obviously blue and black; others only saw it as white and gold.

Caitlin McNeill, a friend of both the bride and groom, couldn't stop thinking about the photo she had seen. She was so curious about the science behind the difference in color perception that she posted the image on her Tumblr account and asked her several thousand followers to help solve the mystery. Little did she know, the photo would go viral overnight. It led to worldwide media exposure and became an Internet phenomenon. Finally, on February 27, 2015, the whole world was divided into two teams: *Team Blue and Black* and *Team White and Gold.*

I was in the office when my colleagues were asking each other about the photo. It was a hilarious moment, because many people were like, "Are you serious? You are not joking or lying to me, right?" The members of both teams were so certain about the colors that they couldn't believe the other team saw them differently. According to a poll by Buzzfeed, over two-thirds of the users responded that the dress was white and gold. But the majority was wrong. The dress was, indeed, blue and black. Cecilia even wore the dress on *The Ellen Show* to confirm the colors and end the controversy. People who attended Grace's wedding and saw the actual dress could also tell the dress was blue and black. So what happened with the photo and our perception?

According to a video by AsapSCIENCE, the lighting in the image was so bad that it created a color constancy illusion for those who only saw the picture. Our brains auto-adjust sensory information, such as colors, to keep them similar under different conditions. We expect something in shadow to appear darker, so our brains compensate for it by making the color look lighter. However, in the case of the dress, our brains couldn't decide if the photo was shot in the open with blue light, or under an artificial yellow light inside in a room, due to a lack of information. The brain has to make assumptions and then interpret the information based on those assumptions. As a result, there were two vastly different color perceptions of the dress.

Perception of reality is not the same as reality. What we interpret is not the same as what we see.

Our brains make assumptions all the time. But what we assume is not always true. It is based on our expectations and past experiences. So we can have the same information and circumstances and yet perceive them differently. Our perception shapes our reality, but it's not actual reality. We might be so certain that we are right and yet still be wrong.

Self-perception works the same way, too. We judge ourselves based on our beliefs and assume that we are unworthy, but how many of these thoughts are actually true?

Most Thoughts Are Biased

In the book *The Art of Thinking Clearly,* author Rolf Dobelli explains the different types of cognitive errors that our minds can possibly make. They include:

- Confirmation Bias: The tendency to interpret new information that confirms our beliefs and filter out information that contradicts our existing views.
- Availability Bias: The tendency to believe

something is true or likely to happen based on the availability of the information in our memory.

- Association Bias: The tendency to link two unrelated things or events together.
- Anchoring: The tendency to rely on the first piece of information we hear to make a decision.
- Contrast Effect: The tendency to make something look better or worse by comparing it with a contrasting object.

For someone with low self-esteem, these biases are going to make overcoming your negative self-talk more challenging. You will have a tendency to find and interpret information to confirm your inferiority and defectiveness (confirmation bias). You are likely to associate your self-worth with events that have nothing to do with you (association bias) and judge yourself based on your negative childhood memories (availability bias). You are also inclined to compare yourself with someone you believe to be better than you (contrast effect) and decide whether something is true or not based on the first piece of information you hear (anchoring).

But where do you first hear this information from?

Your biased mind.

No two situations are the same, regardless how similar they might seem.

We can't perceive ourselves accurately based on our past experiences because we are biased. Just because we had a bad childhood, it doesn't mean that we would, or should, be miserable now. Just because we failed to meet our parents' expectations, it doesn't mean that we are unlovable or a failure. We established most of our self-beliefs during our childhood, but they were based on our limited understanding of the world around us. They are either flawed or have become outdated. We can't take these beliefs at face value anymore.

This applies to positive beliefs, too. Beliefs don't let you see what *is*. We distort the truth whenever we judge the present moment in comparison with something from the past. Believing that you will succeed every single time just because you have a proven record of success makes you complacent.

The truth is everything is impermanent. Nothing stays the same. Flowers wither. Our bodies grow old. Even our thoughts and emotions seem to dissolve over time. When we have a fixed concept of self, we lose ourselves in the past and don't allow ourselves to just *be* who we are in the present.

The Mind Loves Double Standards

Perception doesn't only vary from person to person. An individual can make different judgments on the same matter, too. These double standards come from the contradicting views and beliefs that our subpersonalities have. One of the most obvious examples for people who have low self-esteem is the difference between the way we treat ourselves and the way we treat others.

Most of us don't go around criticizing how bad other people are. When we hear someone do that, we think it's harsh, impolite, and rude. It hurts the other person's feelings. We can relate to this feeling, but when it comes to criticizing ourselves, we do it so frequently and without restraint that we don't even recognize how hard we are on ourselves. How is self-criticism not rude and hurtful to us? Yet, our inner critics continue to attack us relentlessly.

When someone makes a mistake, we are quick to forgive and find an excuse for them. But when we make the same mistake, our inner critics blow everything out of proportion and make us feel guilty, possibly for a long time. We believe these negative thoughts about ourselves, but we don't judge others by the same standards we have for ourselves.

Most of us are much kinder to others than we are to ourselves.

Our perceptions are based on what we want to perceive, and not the truth. The mind has two standards: one for how we treat others and one for how we treat ourselves. Being nice to other people helps us be accepted socially and makes us feel good about ourselves. It serves a purpose. But when it comes to being nice to ourselves, we believe it means we are selfish. So we would rather give and receive love from others than give it to ourselves, even though we have the same capacity to love ourselves.

Having two different standards means that others are always more successful, wealthier, healthier, happier, or somehow better than us. When others earn less than us, we justify it by thinking they have other great things in life, such as relationships and passion, or perhaps we believe they will earn more in the future. When we don't achieve our own goals, we blame ourselves for being lazy, not talented enough, or not taking advantage of the opportunities presented to us. We can never win when we compare ourselves to others because the judging criteria are not the same in the first place. We expect ourselves to be more successful than the people around us, but our standard for ourselves is always much higher than what we have for others. So how can we trust our thoughts when they are so biased and of different standards?

Words Are Just Symbols

In the book *The Fifth Agreement*, the authors tell us to be skeptical of our thoughts, because words are symbols and symbols are not the truth. When you tell yourself: *You aren't good enough,* these words are based on what you *believe* good enough is. "Good enough" to you might mean:

- Taking care of your children's needs
- Being a millionaire
- Having someone who loves and understands you
- Doing something significant that changes the world
- Being liked by everyone

To another person, the words "not good enough" might mean something totally different. Everything we think and believe about ourselves and other people is just an opinion or perspective that we have. It's not the same for everyone. Our self-criticism cannot be true because the same words have different meanings to different people.

Words can't harm you when they don't mean anything to you.

What if someone walked up to you and said, "You are a blue cupboard." Would you believe them or would you be confused by what they said? Now, if another person walked up to you and told you that you are unlovable and worthless, how would you feel?

To be hurt by someone else's words, we must first understand what the words mean. The words, "blue cupboard" have no impact on us because we don't believe that we are blue or a cupboard. Our minds do not assign any special meaning to a blue cupboard. Since there is no file in our belief system that is associated with a blue cupboard, we are more likely to doubt what the other person is saying: *What does he mean by blue cupboard? Does he mean I'm feeling blue? Or does he means I look like a cupboard?*

On the other hand, if our belief systems contain a file that is associated with being unlovable and worthless, the subconscious mind will retrieve the memory of all the times when we felt unworthy and replay these past experiences in our head. Every time we criticize ourselves, we don't feel good about it. But it's not the words that are hurtful – it's the emotions, memories, meanings, and everything else that our minds have attached to the words that affect us.

Again, where do we get our beliefs from?

Through past conditioning.

We learned these symbols from our parents, our siblings, and the society in which we live. If you think you are imperfect, someone must have passed down their knowledge of imperfection to you. When you were a child, you didn't know what perfection was. You were not bothered by it until you learned the word "perfection" from someone else and they told you what it meant to be perfect. Even if your parents did not tell you exactly what perfection was to them, you might have inferred meanings from their actions. When you stored the memory of the word "perfection" in your brain, you also stored your interpretation of what perfection looks and feels like, to be used in the future.

When we feel hurt by our own critical thoughts, it's because we *believe* in the interpretations our minds make. But these interpretations are just mental assumptions made. Unfortunately, the mind is an efficient, meaning-making machine. It has a habit of interpreting information in the same way, even when the meanings it infers are wrong.

Chapter 2

When Self-Criticism Is a Habit

"Habit energy is pushing us. Sometimes we do something without knowing we're doing it. Even when we don't want to do something, we still do it."

— THICH NHAT HANH, YOUR TRUE HOME

William was doing some assignments, and I noticed that whenever he spotted a mistake he would swear some vulgarity at himself. He probably didn't realize he was continually beating himself up, even when he was with me.

William was in his early twenties, and he was the first student I ever had. Whenever I talked to him, he was always polite, but when he talked to himself, it was as though he had been transformed into another person. The first time I saw him behave this way, I was surprised, yet intrigued. I have an inner critic, too, but mine is mostly internal. His inner critic scolds him out loud and sounds much nastier than mine.

As I taught more students, I realized that William wasn't alone in this behavior. One student says, "I'm stupid" whenever she doesn't know how to answer a question. Another student gives the excuse that she's lazy when she doesn't want to do the work. Each of them has a specific trigger that causes them to be self-critical.

Then, there are students who are uptight about answering questions. It's as though something fatal is going to happen to them if they answer incorrectly. These students are probably afraid of feeling shame. So to prevent their ego from hurting, they would rather say they don't know and avoid answering the question at all.

It's easier to observe other people being hard on themselves than to recognize it in ourselves, because self-criticism has already become a habit for most of us. Similar to all the other habits, it has become so ingrained in us that we do it automatically without any conscious effort. We might find ourselves feeling low, unhappy, or lacking in energy all of a sudden, and not realize what causes us to feel this way.

Negative self-talk isn't natural to human beings.

We are not born with an inner critic! Babies don't blame themselves for being "bad." Self-criticism only feels natural after many repetitions.

Efficiency vs. Accuracy

The mind takes shortcuts and makes snap judgments. In his book *Thinking, Fast and Slow,* psychologist Daniel Kahneman describes the two different ways we think:

- System 1 is fast, intuitive, and emotional.
- System 2 is slow, deliberate, and logical.

We have a tendency to rely on System 1 to make judgments, because it requires no mental effort. However, it might cause us to make incorrect, quick judgments based on our past experiences and habits.

Earlier in this book, I mentioned Nelly, who keeps making careless mistakes despite understanding the concepts. For example, she knows that $(a^3)^{-1}$ is equal to, $a^{3\times(-1)}$, which gives the answer, a^{-3}. We have done it together many times. But when she was solving the problem, her mind instantaneously gave her the answer, a^{-2}. Her mind is so used to doing 3 - 1 = 2, that she was quick to believe the first thought that occurred to her. She didn't realize she had made a mistake. If she had developed the habit of slowing down and used System 2 to check on her instinct, she would have spotted her error and corrected the mistake.

Just like Nelly, most of our thoughts (including self-criticism) are automatic and created at the subconscious level. It's easy for us to believe these thoughts because they are most likely the first piece of information we hear.

The subconscious mind is an efficient instrument.

Once it gets used to something, the subconscious mind creates mental shortcuts to produce the same conclusion every single time. It doesn't waste any effort to process the same or similar information again. Sometimes, it even ignores the information it receives that is contrary to our beliefs. This helps us save time, which is great, but the problem is that the subconscious mind doesn't discriminate the good from the bad. Our conscious minds are supposed to do the hard work of discerning.

But most of us don't make the extra effort to question or check what the mind says. To us, our thoughts are reality. We don't separate ourselves from our thoughts. In fact, *we think we are our thoughts*. We trust everything our minds tell us, even though they might be unkind, hurtful, and untrue, and we end up building negative habits like self-criticism.

Once we form a habit, it's difficult to change. Everyone knows that smoking is bad for our health, but there are people who still smoke. Everyone knows we need to save money for a rainy day, but some of us still spend more than we earn. Everyone knows that eating too many sweets and snacks will make us unhealthy, but we still eat them.

Our habitual behaviors don't make any logical sense, but we can't persuade our subconscious minds to be more positive because it doesn't listen to logic and facts. It only cares about efficiency. It sacrifices accuracy for the sake of efficiency. To the mind, performing a habit is efficient, but changing a habit isn't – it requires effort. So once our subconscious minds establish a habit, it's unlikely to change unless we understand what keeps the habit intact.

Why Do We Enjoy Beating Ourselves Up?

According to Charles Duhigg, in his book *The Power of Habit*, the habit loop is a psychological loop that controls all of our habits. Each habit consists of three parts: a cue, a routine, and a reward.

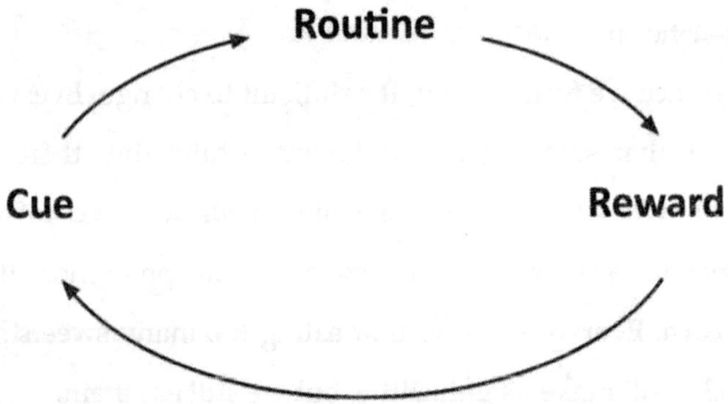

The cue can be anything that triggers the habit. We can have multiple cues for one habit and they can be internal or external. For example, when you see your friends having a great conversation without you (external cue), you might think you aren't good enough for them. Your mind might also trigger the same thought when you are feeling alone at home (internal cue).

Whenever a cue is triggered, we perform a routine that makes us feel satisfied and rewarded. This loop keeps our habits intact. So in William's example, one of his cues for self-criticism might be making mistakes. Whenever he makes a mistake in his assignment (the cue), his mind automatically attacks him for being wrong (the routine), and a part of him feels a sense of relief after being punished (the reward). Once the habit is established, William's mind executes this habit loop without any conscious effort from him.

All our self-criticism habits follow this same habit loop. There must be some cues that trigger your negative self-talk and rewards that drive your mind to attack you. But why would anyone want to feel rewarded by being criticized?

The reward is for the mind, not for us.

Although beating ourselves up makes us feel bad about ourselves, a part of us desires the instant gratification it provides. When the mind gets what it wants, the brain releases some happy chemicals that elevate our mood and ease the tension inside us. They keep our habits intact, drive our automatic behaviors, and keep us wanting more.

Here are three possible incentives for the mind:

1. It affirms our negative self-beliefs.

Once William asked me if I was feeling frustrated because he couldn't understand a concept immediately. From the way he asked, I could tell he wasn't really concerned about how I felt. He was actually seeking confirmation that he is a slow learner. It was a chance for him to validate his self-belief from an outside source.

Being a tutor, I noticed that some students keep wanting to validate their weaknesses. They usually ask me questions such as: *Teacher, am I stupid?*, *Teacher, I'm dumb, right?* or *It's a disgrace to get such a result, right?* When I say, "No" and offer them another perspective, they either disagree or doubt what I've said. Before they asked the question, they already had a preconceived belief about themselves. They are not seeking an answer; their minds are just seeking more evidence to support their identity as someone who is stupid and unworthy.

Negative self-talk offers us some comfort because it's familiar.

We all have negative beliefs about ourselves, but it's easier to see it in others than in ourselves. Self-criticism helps affirm these beliefs and makes our victim identity stronger. It is more comforting than saying something good about ourselves that we don't really believe. This is why people who have low self-esteem resist a compliment. Any praise opposes what they are already certain about with regard to themselves. They have perceived themselves as unworthy for a long time, often since childhood. Accepting a compliment weakens the victim identity that the subconscious mind has spent years building.

An opposing point of view also means more work for the subconscious mind. If you strongly believe that you are unworthy, the mind doesn't need to reexamine and revise your self-concept anymore – you are unworthy. The decision has been made. But if you have doubts, the mind has to ascertain the accuracy of the new information. It has to work! As mentioned before, its preference is to be efficient and energy-saving. It wants to keep the old shortcuts and patterns the same. The stronger our belief system gets and the fewer doubts we have, the less work the mind needs to do.

2. It is used for self-discipline and motivation.

An acquaintance once told me that his greatest enemy is himself. He is a very ambitious guy who has high expectations for himself. He believes that self-criticism will result in success, and he thinks that people who are too nice to themselves are being dishonest. They are just giving themselves false assurance that they are good enough.

There are many people like him who believe that self-criticism will make them happier and more successful. Even though they feel miserable about talking to themselves in a mean way, they still feel like it's helpful. But how true is this?

To a certain extent, self-criticism and punishment help us regulate our actions and behaviors. They protect us from harm by helping us remember past pain, so we will stay away from things that cause us the pain. For example, we would rather punish ourselves than fail publicly, be rejected by others, or be punished by law. This is how our parents kept us from doing something socially unacceptable. They forced us to do what they wanted us to do, and so we learned this tactic from them.

**Criticism might get us to change,
but it is not required.**

Self-regulation skills are definitely necessary to control impulses and cope with social norms and rules. However, we don't have to be harsh towards ourselves in order to control our behaviors. There is no correlation between success and self-criticism. William still makes mistakes despite swearing at himself. People aren't successful because they criticize themselves. Their success comes from adopting the right strategies and habits. We can be kind and compassionate towards ourselves and also achieve our goals.

The reason why some adults still use self-criticism to discipline themselves is that they lack self-trust. They don't believe they will take the right action when they are left on their own. Instead of being responsible for their own actions and deciding what's best for themselves, they still need someone else (*i.e.*, their parents in the past and now the inner critic) to push them to do what's right and tell them what they can or cannot do.

Habitual self-criticism is rewarding for the mind. As long as you continue to believe that being critical makes you better, it allows the mind to control your actions by hooking you in with higher expectations for yourself.

3. It makes us pay for our mistakes.

Self-criticism sometimes serves as a form of self-punishment, and punishment is a reward in itself. When we beat ourselves up, we feel less guilty about the mistakes we have made. It momentarily reduces our emotional pain. Isn't this what most of us experienced when we were young?

When we did something wrong, our parents would punish us, but eventually, they would forgive us. At first, we would feel bad about making a mistake, but we knew that everything would go back to normal *after* we were punished. Self-punishment works the same way. We punish ourselves because there is a part of us that thinks we deserve it and we are at fault. Scolding ourselves makes us pay for our mistakes and gives us the permission to move on. It helps us resolve some of the negative feelings, such as shame and guilt, that are hidden deep down inside of us.

Self-punishment makes us feel our feelings instead of running away from them.

If you have feelings or deep-seated beliefs of unworthiness and inferiority, self-criticism can help you bring these feelings to the surface so you can experience them fully and not continue ignoring their existence.

However, this makes the victim identity stronger. Also, when it becomes a habit, we end up criticizing ourselves even more and focus too much on our weaknesses. You don't need to criticize yourself in order to feel these emotions. Again, there is no correlation between the two.

How to Change a Habit

Now that you understand the habit mechanism better, here are a few ways to change a habit.

First, you can avoid the cues that trigger your self-criticism. Suppose you have friends who always make you feel bad about yourself – you can choose to hang out with them less. However, avoidance is not always possible. If making mistakes is one of the cues, you can't avoid making mistakes forever. You are bound to make a mistake someday. Plus, you will end up designing your life around the self-criticism habit just so you don't make any mistakes. Obviously, this is not a very good idea.

Second, you can withhold or remove the rewards from your mind. That's what many people do. Your mind wants affirmation that you are bad, but you disallow it. Instead, you feed your mind with positive affirmations. If you have any negative beliefs, you try to rephrase them into positive ones. When your inner critic wants to force you to do better or makes you feel some of your emotions, you ignore it and shut it off. This is okay for a while, but it might backfire or exhaust you when you spend too much of your energy preventing your mind from getting what it wants. Withholding the rewards doesn't stop the mind from wanting them.

Third, as suggested by Charles Duhigg, is to change the routine. Replace self-criticism with another routine that supports both the cues and the rewards. Perhaps you have already noticed that you can't control the thoughts created by your subconscious mind. You might be doing something simple like brushing your teeth, and your mind is simultaneously thinking about a million other things, ranging from what to do next to how miserable your life is. It's tough to replace the self-criticism routine with something else because the mind is on autopilot most of the time.

Don't change your self-criticism habit.
Change your habitual reactions to self-criticism.

However, we can control our habitual reactions. We can replace our current reactions with a new routine so that even when we have critical thoughts, we will know how to deal with them. This allows the mind to continue getting its rewards and not affect us. Changing our reaction will also eventually reduce our self-criticism, even though this isn't the main objective.

Before we learn how to change our reactions to self-criticism, let's understand how we are reacting to it now.

Chapter 3

Your Reaction Matters

> *"You can't stop negative thoughts from popping into your head, but you can choose to stop letting them control you and your life."*
>
> — LORI DESCHENE, FOUNDER OF TINYBUDDHA

Knock, knock. It's the mailman again. This is the fifteenth time he has knocked on your front door today. He has been bringing you registered letters from a person called "Inner Critic" for the past few years. You have read the message in the letters before and you know how nasty and critical they are.

What should you do? Let's answer this question by using several people as examples:

The first person, **Angry Man**, decided to fight and resist receiving such mail. When the mailman came, he told him to go away. But the mailman wouldn't stop knocking on his door until he accepted the mail. That's his job – to deliver the letters. So Angry Man went to the Inner Critic's house. He threatened him and told him not to send any more letters. But the Inner Critic didn't care; he continued to send the letters just because he could. He had paid for the postage stamps and he believed that what he had written was the truth. Angry Man was frustrated. He didn't want to receive any more mail from the Inner Critic but he didn't know what to do about it.

The second person, **Mrs. Denial**, chose to escape from her problem. She ran away from home so she would never receive the letters. If no one is home, the mail can't be delivered, right? Somehow the mailman was able to track her down no matter where she went. He was there at the bar when she was drowning her sorrows with an alcoholic drink. He was there at the casino when she was distracting herself with the slot machine. Mrs. Denial felt so pestered by the mailman that she even tried to deny her identity: *No, I'm not Mrs. Denial. These letters aren't for me.* But it didn't work. The mailman's job is to deliver the letters. He makes sure all the letters are delivered to the right person.

The third person, **Ms. Worry**, received the letters from the mailman, but she was obsessed with them. She kept reading them over and over again. The more she read the letters, the more worried she became: *What if the letter is right? What if I never amount to anything? What if I can't be wealthy? What if no one loves me? What if other people get ahold of these letters? Will they find out about my flaws, too?*

Ms. Worry couldn't let go of her negative thoughts. In fact, she conjured up more negative thoughts and started blaming others for her misfortune: *Why do I have to receive this mail? Why did the mailman deliver such letters to me? Why does the Inner Critic send me such mail? Why me?* Ms. Worry felt really helpless and couldn't focus on anything except the critical letters.

The last person, **Helpless Child**, cried whenever she received a letter. She believed everything that was written in them. She locked herself inside the house and wallowed in self-pity. Just like Ms. Worry, she kept the letters safe, as if they were treasures, and she reread them time and time again. But unlike Ms. Worry, she didn't even try to resist the criticism contained within them. She just accepted that she wasn't good enough and there was nothing she could do about it. She hated herself for being so weak. Each letter dictated her mood for the rest of the day, the rest of the week, or perhaps the rest of her life.

The Four Common Reactions to Self-Criticism

The opening story in this chapter captures the four common reactions to self-criticism: fight, escape, ruminate, and resign. I've reacted in each of these ways at least once in my lifetime. However, we usually have one reaction that we habitually exhibit when our inner critic attacks us.

Some of us prefer to ruminate on the issue, while others want so badly to silence the inner critic. There are also some of us who use distractions to numb ourselves to self-criticism – others simply resign themselves to their fate and let the inner critic continue to cause pain.

Our reaction to self-criticism is more important than the self-criticism itself.

Paying attention to our reactions is very important because the only thing we have control over is how we react. This also provides an opportunity to practice mindfulness. By being aware of our reactions, we can change the way we normally react to our negative self-talk and free ourselves from unnecessary turmoil. Even if we don't change our reactions, or we are not sure how to, at least we can see how self-criticism causes us to act in a certain way and understand why our current reactions are ineffective in dealing with our problems.

The following is a discussion about how we usually react to self-criticism. Identify your most common reaction, and we will discuss alternatives in the next chapter.

1. Rumination

This is probably the most destruction reaction of all. Not only will you fail in silencing your inner critic, you will get more deeply stuck in your problems. The mind's habit is to spot and solve problems. When you ruminate, it seems as though you are solving the problem, but, in reality, you are just dwelling on the problem and making it worse. When we ruminate, we are not looking for solutions; we are looking for possible causes and consequences. We ask "why" questions such as:

- Why can't I do this?
- Why did I make a mistake?
- Why do I keep failing?
- Why did he or she do this to me?
- Why am I so stupid?

Seldom, do we ask "what," "who," or "how" questions

such as:

- What can I do to make the situation better?
- What are the possible solutions to my problem?
- Who can I talk to?
- Who can help me with my problem?
- How can I look at my trouble from a different angle?

The reason for this is simple. We don't know how to solve the problem and we feel helpless. So by asking "why" questions, we take away the pain of not knowing the solutions. It allows us to attribute some kind of reason to our issues and blame others or our circumstances for it. It gives us some relief from our distress and makes us feel better when we sympathize with ourselves in difficult situations.

However, rumination is unhealthy. It can easily lead to self-hatred, depression, and anxiety. In *The Emotional Gift,* I wrote about how my depression was triggered when I kept asking questions such as," *Why didn't the animation studio founder keep his promise?* and *Why didn't he hire me like he promised he would?* Initially, I tried to ask myself "what" questions: *What can I do to get some income?* But I was so focused on finding the cause of the problem that I couldn't see any solution at the time. I soon went back to asking why and finding someone or something to blame.

Asking why can help you in a different scenario, but it's ineffective when you are in a downward spiral.

My mind started to get stuck in an unhealthy, repetitive loop. Whenever I asked why I had been betrayed, my inner critic received new fuel to bash me with for being naive, worthless, and inferior. Then my self-criticism triggered me to think: *Why am I so dumb?* and this resulted in even more negative self-talk.

Here's another example. One of my students, Sharon, loves to say she's stupid when she can't solve mathematics problems. Sometimes, she gets so tired of doing difficult questions that she makes a scene and asks a lot of rhetorical questions such as *Why do we have examinations?*, *Who invented math?*, and *Why do we need to study math?* Asking these questions is meaningless. They don't help reduce her stress, at all, or help her answer the mathematics problems. Yes, perhaps the current education system isn't effective. But asking questions when you have no power to change the system will only make you feel more angry and helpless. These questions should be asked by the people who have the power to change the education system, or at least the ability to influence change. Instead of running away from her stress, she needs to accept the current education system as it is now and do her best to work with what she has been given.

Rumination doesn't help us take action to resolve our difficulties. We try to solve problems in our heads but end up hurting ourselves. When we blame others or ourselves for our misery, we are not taking responsibility for our problems. Unfortunately, rumination is a habit that most of us have developed to cope with self-criticism. To overcome this habit, we must pay more attention to the questions we ask ourselves and take actions that move us forward.

2. Resignation

Surrendering to our self-criticism is not a bad solution. At least, it is better than worrying and over-analyzing the situation. There is less internal conflict in your mind and less resentment towards the people and events in your life when you choose to be accepting.

Similar to the mailman, the job of the subconscious is

to bring you information that is relevant to you at any given moment. Its job is not to help you filter the messages, so resisting it is futile. It's better to receive the critical thoughts without any resistance and accept that our minds have stored negative beliefs about ourselves.

The problem doesn't lie with the critical thoughts. It lies with what we choose to believe in.

The difference between resignation and disbelief is that people who resign in the face of self-criticism trust what their inner critics say.

However, people who disbelieve *listen without believing*. Both types of people accept the message the inner critic is trying to convey, but the way they react to the criticism is different. The former doesn't understand the mechanism of the subconscious mind and believes he or she *is* their mind, and that whatever the mind tells them must be true. The latter knows that their minds and their true selves are separated. They know the subconscious mind acts automatically, based on habits, past experiences, and beliefs, so the critical thoughts they hear from the inner critic might not be true. They understand that each thought only represents one perspective and they are willing to explore other views.

The good thing about resignation, though, is that it allows you to feel your sorrow and despair. When I was in secondary school, I often felt alone and sad about not being able to connect deeply with the other students. I envied the students who were getting along great with each other. I *accepted* the situation and didn't do much about my low self-esteem, other than writing small notes to myself and burying them in the ground. When my inner critic told me that no one liked me, I felt hurt, but I was never depressed. Even though I believed what the inner critic told me, I was in touch with my feelings and able to let them go on a regular basis. So it didn't escalate into something unmanageable.

Resignation is the reaction I used during most of my school life in order to cope with self-criticism. Although it didn't add mental noise or create internal turmoil, it strengthened my negative self-beliefs. The more I believed what my inner critic told me, the more I felt inferior and disconnected from the world.

Accepting and feeling your emotions is good. However, if we spend too much time exploring our negative feelings, it takes away the time and energy we need to create positive changes in our lives. Even when there is an opportunity for growth, we might be so used to feeling powerless that we don't believe change is possible.

3. Escape

Escape is probably the most common reaction to combat our inner critic. Most of the time, we don't even realize we are distracting ourselves from self-criticism. There are many ways to escape. We can numb our feelings and thoughts with entertainment, games, TV, food, alcohol, drug, fantasy, and sex.

When we feel incompetent in our work and abilities, most people would rather procrastinate by watching random videos or playing games online than work. When our relationships are not going well, instead of blaming ourselves, we might use food to give us some comfort. When we have done something wrong that we can't forgive ourselves for, alcohol might be the choice for some people to forget their problems. Anything that distracts us from our critical thoughts can be used as a form of escape. Even meditation can be a form of escape.

If you truly understand the essence of mindfulness practice, you know that mindfulness is not about escaping problems. In mindfulness meditation, we face our difficulties and accept what we are feeling at the moment. We are not running away from it. However, some of us use meditation to escape reality. Even though escaping might be an effective strategy to tune out the noise inside our heads, we are actually giving up our power to our minds. We are indirectly letting our minds influence our behaviors and run our lives.

Distractions aren't all bad. They can help us avoid pain and relentless attacks from the inner critic, especially when we don't know how to deal with it. Blocking out unhappy memories can help people cope with their traumatic experiences. Not only does this offer a kind of relief, it's a survival mechanism for some people. There are also times when we truly need to relax and enjoy simple pleasures, such as entertainment and food.

Escaping is only harmful when we are addicted to it and unconscious we are doing it.

The key differences between relaxation and escaping are enjoyment and freedom of choice. Are we doing what we really want to do, right now? Do we feel bad after doing the activity? Eckhart Tolle, a spiritual teacher, says "Addiction begins with pain and ends with pain." When you are escaping your problems, you will continue to feel pain after the activity ends. You can run away from your inner critic for a while, but you can't run away from it forever. You will still have to face your issues someday.

My student, Shane, uses his imagination to prevent himself from feeling unworthy for failing his examinations. He always dreams about how nice it would be if there was no school, or he imagines he's in some kind of alternate reality. However, escaping is not a long-term solution. It only delays the problem. Shane still needs to find a way to pass his examinations. Otherwise, he won't be promoted to the next level. The problem doesn't go away on its own.

Furthermore, the same activity that we used to escape from the inner critic might trigger the inner critic to attack us in another way. For example, you might eat snacks when you feel incompetent at work. But after you enjoy the snack, the inner critic makes you feel guilty for eating too much unhealthy food. No matter where you turn, the inner critic is there to make you feel bad about yourself.

When we are truly relaxing, we focus on the enjoyment the activity brings. We are conscious and choose to do only the things we truly want to do. There were times when I unknowingly used the TV as a distraction to escape from a difficult task. When I caught myself doing this, I realized I was watching some mindless TV program that I didn't even enjoy watching. I was only watching it because I didn't want to face my inner critic.

If you are doing something that you are not obligated to do and you are not enjoying yourself, it's a telltale sign you are avoiding or ignoring a deeper issue. If you repeatedly use an activity to avoid your inner critic, it will soon become an addiction or another bad habit. You will feel an urge to perform the undesirable activity even when you don't want to, so it's best to use distractions sparingly.

4. Fight

Some of us resist the pain inflicted by the inner critic by trying to stop or silence our minds from scolding us. We feel the pain as a victim, but instead of accepting our negative thoughts, we decide to fight against them.

There are two ways of fighting. The first way is the polite way. You try to eliminate the mental noises in your head by replacing and correcting them with positive thoughts or affirmations. You convince your mind that what it says about you is wrong and biased, and you try to change your subconscious beliefs about yourself. The second way is to use force. You treat your inner critic like an enemy and feel angry when it attacks you. You try to stop the criticism by lashing out towards your mind. Some of us started the first way, but we soon became frustrated when it didn't work, and we ended up using the second method.

The problem with the first way is that it creates dissonance. For those of us with low self-esteem, who don't believe positive thoughts about ourselves, it might make us feel worse. When we keep comparing our current, negative perception of ourselves with the ideal self we desire, we are constantly reminded of what a bad person we are now. Even though positive affirmations have some merit, and neuroplasticity research has shown that the brain can be changed, it takes time and conscious effort to change your beliefs. With positive thinking, you might feel happy about yourself temporarily. But soon, the negative thoughts will intrude into your mind again when you are distracted or unaware and make you give up any hope of being positive.

Positive thinking needs to be supported by positive experiences and feelings. The emotional brain doesn't listen to logic. No matter how your rational brain tries to convince your emotional brain, it's a losing battle. You can't stop your subconscious from having negative thoughts. Arguing with your subconscious will only create more chaos in your head, increase resistance, and produce more negative feelings.

Forcing yourself to accept positive thoughts when your mind isn't ready never works.

Sharon, the same student from the rumination example above, started telling herself she is clever after I shared with her the impact of negative self-talk. But the way she praised herself was so inauthentic it sounded like she was mocking herself. I had to ask her to stop, because the more she said, "I am clever," the more she sounded like she was affirming her stupidity.

Positive thinking doesn't work unless it's believable. You can't trade your belief of "no one loves me" with "everyone loves me." You are just deceiving yourself. If you are still holding onto the belief that you are not good enough, you can't just chuck it aside and go for the positive thoughts. The underlying negative feeling will still be there. You are depriving your mind of its rewards. The mind wants the negative beliefs to be affirmed, but you give it something that totally contradicts what was stored inside your brain instead. If you are new to changing your beliefs, you would be better off taking a neutral stand (*i.e.* you are neither good nor bad) rather than swinging from one extreme to another or fighting with your inner critic.

When you fight your inner critic, you are sending two messages to your brain. One, you believe what the mind says about you is true. If you don't believe what the inner critic says is true, why do you need to defend it? Remember the "blue cupboard" example in Chapter 1? When you don't believe you are a blue cupboard, you won't care if your inner critic calls you a blue cupboard or not.

Second, you are rejecting the message that the inner critic gives you. You are judging the inner critic and making it an enemy. Even though the tone of your inner critic is harsh or mean, it might have some valuable information to offer. It's like our parents; they had good intentions for us but communicated the message poorly.

The inner critic isn't an enemy.

Even if the interpretation is inaccurate, there's no need to suppress your inner critic. It's just one of the people living inside your head. All of them have different ideas and perceptions about how you should live. You, the true self, have to decide who to listen to and then lead your subpersonalities, not the other way round. There's no need to isolate any of them. When you can't accept both your negative and positive thoughts, you become vulnerable to inner conflict.

Chapter 4

What Is and What Isn't Disbelieving?

"Don't mind criticism. If it is untrue, disregard it; if it is fair; keep from irritation; if it is ignorant, smile; if it is justified, it is not a criticism, learn from it."

— ANONYMOUS

Knock, knock. It's the mailman again. You have another registered letter from the Inner Critic. Instead of rejecting the letter, you accept the letter gladly and thank the mailman for the delivery.

Before you read the letter, you take a deep breath and remove any mental noises in your head. This time you are prepared to accept the message gracefully. No more dwelling on the letter. No more escaping. You are going to face the message bravely, but you are not going to assume that everything in the letter is true.

As you read the letter, a part of you still feels uneasy and hurt. However, instead of pitying yourself, this time you are aware of the emotions in your body. You allow them to simply be there for a while and truly feel your feelings. When you are ready, you let them go. The letter has done its job – you throw it into the rubbish bin and continue with your life.

This is the art of disbelieving.

Living in a house with too many unresolved letters (*i.e.*, mental conflicts) is suffocating. When we were young, we didn't receive a lot of mail. We believed every letter we received was important and we accepted everything without filtering. Now that we are adults, our minds have become cluttered with too many letters. We have a choice to keep or throw them away. After you receive a letter and read it, you get to decide whether you need to keep it, or not. If you decide *not* to keep it or act on the information it contains, simply tear it up and throw it away once it has delivered the message. We don't keep all our letters, anyway, so why hold onto our self-criticism?

Disbelief Isn't Self-Denial

Some people – especially those who have high expectations for themselves – think that disbelieving critical thoughts is self-deception. Like the acquaintance I mentioned in Chapter 2, they believe that when you don't recognize your own flaws and imperfections, you are living in denial. But that's not what disbelief is about.

When you make a mistake and your inner critic calls you stupid, disbelieving this critical thought doesn't mean you ignore the fact that you made a mistake. The word "stupid" is a judgment. It's an opinion your subconscious mind makes about you for making a mistake. The belief that you are stupid is a conclusion based on your interpretation of all the mistakes you have made in the past. It's not the truth. Someone can be clever and yet make mistakes. There is no correlation between the two. The only truth in this situation is that you made a mistake, so correct the mistake. End of story.

Here's another example. You texted your friend and he didn't reply for days. What does your mind do? It starts to look for reasons why your friend hasn't texted you back: *Perhaps he is busy and forgot to reply. Maybe he is away for a holiday or business trip.* It could be your friend doesn't know what to say to you after reading your message. Your inner critic concludes that your friend doesn't like you and you are quick to believe it. But is this accurate? It could be, but you *don't know for sure* that it is. Believing your friend doesn't like you is just an assumption your mind made and the assumption can be wrong. The only truth in this situation is that you texted your friend and he didn't reply. Any additional opinions you have on the matter are pure fiction, not facts.

**Escaping is running away from the truth,
but disbelief is running towards the truth.**

Disbelief is about separating the facts from the fiction. When you don't trust your inner critic too quickly, you buy yourself some time to be curious and examine all the facts in any situation. Most, if not all, of our self-criticism, is a lie. Any judgment we have about ourselves is an opinion based on the interpretation of our biased minds. It is a distorted story we tell ourselves, and it becomes our reality when we believe it.

Disbelieving self-judgment doesn't mean we ignore our weaknesses and pretend we are perfect. It just means we don't fall for our own exaggerated story. We still recognize the fact that we make mistakes and fall short of our expectations, but we don't have to judge ourselves for it.

Disbelief Is About Being Open

Disbelief doesn't mean that we don't listen to our thoughts. In fact, it means being open and listening without judgment. Listening doesn't imply that we must believe what we hear. We listen for the purpose of gathering information; we don't listen for the sake of believing and forming an opinion. The information can be true or false, and it's only through mindful listening that we can tell the truth apart from the lies.

When we resign ourselves to self-criticism, not only do we believe what the inner critic says about us, we are also siding with the victim subpersonality. A part of us was hurt by our past experiences and wants to bring us back to those bad memories. There is nothing wrong with caring for yourself when you feel hurt. However, beliefs such as "I'm not good enough" or "No one likes me" are misinterpretations from the past. We don't have to believe them anymore.

When you disbelieve, you don't side with any of your

subpersonalities. You welcome all your thoughts and embrace both the positive and the negative polarities. You take in all views before choosing the path you want to take. The path might be something that one of your subpersonalities has suggested, or it might be nothing like the views provided. The key is that you give all your subpersonalities a chance to relate their messages and be heard, but you make the final decision. You are steering the wheel. Listening to a thought doesn't mean you have to believe the thought or let it dictate what you must do. This is unlike when you hastily believe one of your subpersonalities and let your mind steer your life automatically.

Don't judge your subpersonalities, especially your inner critic.

The important thing about openness is that you don't judge any of your subpersonalities as being good or bad. You don't see your inner critic as the enemy just because it delivers unpleasant messages. You want to understand its point of view and see where it is coming from. Just like an overly-optimistic voice can bring you harm, the inner critic can also bring you constructive information that will help you transform your life. So there's no need to fight or resist the inner critic. Just listen and be curious about what it has to share.

The mind is harmless. Our thoughts can either serve us well or cause us to suffer, depending on the timing and the context. Even though most thoughts are biased, they are only harmful when we choose to believe and react to them mindlessly. When your mind offers creative ideas, you listen to the suggestions, but you don't act on all of them, do you? So why take your critical thoughts so seriously? They are nothing other than comments.

Disbelief Is About Acceptance

When you have a critical thought about yourself, you don't blame yourself for conceiving the thought. You also don't blame others for making you think this way or your parents for making you feel unworthy.

People who disbelieve their thoughts accept that their minds generate negative thoughts sometimes. They know that once a critical thought emerges, it simply is what it is. There's nothing they can do to change the fact that the critical thought is already there. However, they know that they have the power to choose how to react and what to believe. They understand these intrusive thoughts can help them build a stronger mindfulness habit. So they take full responsibility for what they can control, instead of blaming themselves for something they have little or no control over, the subconscious mind.

Disbelieving is different from the other three reactions: ruminating, escaping, and fighting. Unlike these reactions, you don't resist your critical thoughts. You acknowledge and accept their existence. You don't run away from your self-criticism, pretend it's not there, make it go away, complain about it, or join in the criticism. You listen to the message and observe how your body reacts. If it's not the truth, you discard it. You don't hold on to it.

To resist is not to hear.
To disbelieve is to hear.

To listen and understand a message fully, you need to accept what has been said and receive it as a gift. But first, you must free your hands to receive it. Similarly, the practice of disbelieving requires you to free yourself from beliefs. It requires you to take a neutral stand when hearing the message. When you listen with a preconceived notion that something is negative or that you won't like it, you are actually not listening to it; you are judging it. You are just pretending to listen and waiting for your chance to say, *No, this doesn't apply to me.* Your perception gets clouded by your beliefs, and the real wisdom and insights that you possess cannot come forth into your consciousness.

Only when you accept the message from the inner critic completely can you extract the true value from it and apply the lessons learned for the future. Suppose your inner critic tells you that you don't deserve love. This creates an opportunity for you to observe whether any part of your body feels uncomfortable with this criticism. If your body feels hurt by the criticism, there's a part of you that feels unloved and needs to be attended to. This is a reminder to practice self-love. However, if you choose to resist this message from your inner critic and suppress your feelings, you will miss these subtle pieces of information provided by your body and ignore the part of you that is calling for help. You will not hear the real message your mind is trying to deliver.

Disbelief Isn't Self-Doubt

Perhaps you are confused. Does disbelief create more self-doubt? If you can't trust your own thoughts, aren't you doubting yourself?

Doubting your thoughts isn't the same as doubting yourself because you are not your thoughts. In my book, *Empty Your Cup,* I've mentioned that there is a separation between our true selves and our minds. We have a mind, but we are not our minds. We have thoughts, but we are not our thoughts. We are actually the awareness perceiving the thoughts. Some people call this perceiver the *spirit;* some called it the *higher consciousness* or the *higher Self.* The mind generates the thoughts; the perceiver observes the thoughts. When you disbelieve, you are doubting the thoughts, you are not doubting yourself – you are just the perceiver.

Self-doubt is the belief that you can't do something.

Furthermore, self-doubt is a lack of confidence in your abilities. It's the belief that you can't do something. But unlike the victim subpersonality, it doesn't evaluate your self-worth; it evaluates your ability to do something. When you doubt yourself, you can ask rhetorical questions such as:

- What if people don't like me?
- What if I can't do it?
- Am I making the right decision?

You ask these questions not because you are interested in knowing the answer. You ask them because you don't trust your own ability to do something. Deep down inside, you *believe* that you will make a wrong decision and you will experience either regret or failure. When you ask yourself these questions, you are actually seeking validation to support the belief that you can't do something. So how is this disbelieving?

If you feel conflicted and unable to act, it's because the different subpersonalities inside your head are confusing you with their opposing views. Perhaps you feel they all make sense and you are not sure who to listen to. You question which one is right. Instead of taking responsibility and making a decision, you let your subpersonalities fight it out for themselves.

Disbelieving is different. When you disbelieve, you listen to all the views without believing everything you hear and then make a decision. You are skeptical towards all views, not just one particular view. Once you have decided, you go ahead and take action. You don't doubt or second-guess your decision anymore – but not because you believe or know for sure that your decision is the right one, but because you take responsibility for your decision. Even if the outcome is not exactly what you want, you know you can always change your approach and alter your path. This is the difference between disbelieving and self-doubt.

PART TWO

How Can We Learn to Disbelieve?

Changing a habit can be challenging. We might be aware that our behaviors are causing us to suffer. However, we still follow through with our habits because we are so used to them or we don't know what to do otherwise. For example, you might know your addiction to gaming is just a way to escape feeling unworthy, but you continue to play because you don't know how to stop. So the easy way out would be to do something you are already comfortable with: gaming.

Having a plan is important. It gives us something to follow when our habits strike again. This is especially useful when we start a new habit and have a tendency to forget the steps. If we don't plan something to replace our reactions in advance, most of us will take the easy way out and react in habitual ways when we have self-critical thoughts. Therefore, it's best to have a plan ready so you know exactly what to do when you become too hard on yourself again.

To replace any habit, you need to be consistent.

For your mind to adopt the new disbelief habit, you must practice it regularly so your brain forms new neural pathways for the new habit and weakens the old one. As with any habit, the more you do it, the easier it will get.

In the next few chapters, you will find the process I use to change my reactions to self-criticism. I call it the "Disbelief Process." Within each step, there are suggested actions you can take. You can follow the same actions as mine, but I recommend you choose and customize a little according to what suits you best.

Chapter 5

Step #1: Be Aware of Your Thoughts

> *"The primary cause of unhappiness is never the situation but thought about it. Be aware of the thoughts you are thinking."*
>
> — ECKHART TOLLE, A NEW EARTH

"Some women can make that work. But you? You've no charm. You're just fat and ordinary," a lady told another lady in the cafe.

This statement is from the introduction for the Dove France's commercial, *One Beautiful Thought,* which was shown in 2015. In this commercial, the producers get several French ladies to write down in their notebook whenever they have a thought about their looks. The producers then turned those thoughts into a script for two actresses to perform. They invited the unsuspecting ladies back for coffee so they could overhear the actresses repeat their original conversation at the next table.

While listening to the conversation of the actresses, the ladies realized their written thoughts were being spoken out loud. They were shocked and horrified by how violent and harsh their inner thoughts sounded when spoken by another person. It was so awful that some of them had to interrupt the conversation and tell the actress to stop.

The video commercial ended with this powerful message:

"If it's not acceptable to say it to someone else, why say it to ourselves?"

This video not only shows us how hurtful and critical our thoughts can get, it shows us how oblivious we are to self-criticism. If we don't take stock of our thoughts and present them externally, we might not even know how harsh or insidious our inner critics can be. Out of nowhere, a seemingly harmless comment or question from our minds might:

- Stop us from pursuing our dreams

- Keep us in an abusive relationship
- Crush our self-confidence
- Make us feel guilty, lonely, and unloved
- Create unnecessary fear and doubts

If we are aware of our critical thoughts, we can do something about them. But the problem is that most of us don't notice our thoughts. Our minds generate thoughts so quickly that we just believe and act on them immediately, before we are totally conscious of them.

Awareness is all you need.

Being aware of your thoughts is the first and the most important step in the Disbelief Process. To disbelieve your thoughts, you must first be aware of them. If you only have time to master one step, this is the one. Just by noticing your thoughts, you can significantly reduce the noise in your head. Try it out for yourself now. Grab a pen and a piece of paper, and for the next five minutes write down whatever thoughts come to your mind.

What is your experience? Are there more thoughts after the five minutes, or is there a period of no thoughts before the time is up? Are the thoughts repetitive or unique?

If you are like most people, you will find that your stream of thoughts is repetitive and tapers off by the end of five minutes. When you observe your mind, it becomes quieter. It has nothing much to say. However, it's not always easy to remain alert, especially when you are actively involved in doing something else.

Before we explore some actions we can take to become more aware of our thoughts, let's discuss the challenges that keep us from being more aware.

Why Are We Unaware of Our Self-Criticism?

If you are reading this book, you are probably aware of your negative self-talk and the impact it brings, to a certain extent, but are you aware of it every time it arises? Here are two reasons why we are unaware of our tendency to be self-critical.

1. Self-criticism is subtle and elusive.

As I was taking a break from writing this chapter, I went to my fridge and grabbed a chocolate bar. I couldn't open it easily, so I automatically reached for the pair of scissors on my left. At that moment, I was amazed. I was standing there without any conscious thoughts and I noticed my left hand leaving the chocolate bar and reaching out for the pair of scissors. It happened in a split second. I didn't tell my hand to move. There wasn't any verbal command from my mind. *Why did my hand move?* Even though I know the subconscious mind controls our habitual behaviors, I was in awe when my hand moved automatically, without my consciously controlling it.

This got me thinking: *what are thoughts exactly?* One study estimates that we have an average of 70,000 thoughts a day. If you do the math, that's 0.8 thought per second. How is this even possible? You can't even complete a sentence within a second. Whether you believe this study or not, it doesn't matter. It all depends on how you define thoughts.

A thought isn't just words.
It can also be an image or a signal to do something.

Thoughts aren't just created by our conscious thinking. The subconscious mind creates thoughts, too, and sometimes these thoughts are so subtle that it is difficult for us to recognize them. When I was trying to open the chocolate bar, the neurons in my brain were probably transmitting these messages non-verbally:

- *Hey, this doesn't open.*
- *What should I do?*
- *Go get a pair of scissors.*
- *Where are the scissors?*
- *They are on your left.*

The brain processes all this information in less than a second, and within that second it also retrieves memories of the times when I solved similar problems, the image of the scissors, and where it was placed. It's tough for us to notice our self-criticism because the subconscious mind operates the same, efficient way with negative self-talk. It's fast, it's frequent, and it's habitual. You saw someone who is more successful than you on social media and before you realized it, you felt bad about yourself. There might not even be any verbal thoughts about how bad you are. It could be just an image or a memory of the time when you felt low after being compared to your siblings or classmates. The first time you experienced something like this, you might have analyzed it slowly, but the more frequently your mind interprets similar situations in a negative light, it becomes automatic.

Our inner critics hurt us the most when they are subtle. A few casual remarks such as: *Why can't you be like him?*, *Your relationship won't last,* and *Do you think you can do it?* can lure us into self-pity or cause us to engage in unconscious, self-destructive actions.

2. We identify with our self-criticism.

Eckhart Tolle once said, "If you aren't aware of it, you are it." Another reason why it's so challenging to be aware of self-criticism is that we don't maintain a separation between our true selves and the voices in our heads. We identify with our subconscious thoughts as though that's who we are.

For example, if you have a car, you and your car are separate. Even though your car might be giving you problems, you are not the car. It's the same with awareness and the mind. They are separate, but because they are within us and we can't see them clearly, they look as though they are one unit.

It's difficult to see your thoughts
when you are in your thoughts.

You need to step away from your thoughts in order to

see them clearly. If you put this book too close to your face, you can't read the book. The words will lose focus. Just like you need to pull yourself away to read the book, you need to maintain a space between yourself and your thoughts to become aware of them.

This is why it's difficult to notice self-criticism and much easier to recognize when other people criticize and judge you. You can see the damage when the critic is outside of you, but you can't see the difference when you are too close to your thoughts.

Furthermore, some of us see self-criticism as a necessary means to self-discipline. Instead of recognizing our subconscious thoughts as automatic and conditioned, we partake in the criticism, thinking it's good for us. We don't make the effort to be aware of our thoughts.

Most of us are only aware of our self-criticism when it becomes too harsh for us to bear, or when someone else points out to us that we are too hard on ourselves. How can we be more aware of our thoughts on our own?

How Can We Achieve Deeper Awareness?

First and foremost, it's not feasible to sit, meditate, and listen to all our 70,000 thoughts every day. I'm not asking you to do this because this is not awareness. Awareness is not about putting all your focus on your thoughts. It's to acknowledge the existence of your thoughts. It's light, like a bubble, and not as intense as concentrating on something specific. It's like when someone sends a message to your mobile phone to inform you of something and you reply "noted." You acknowledge the message, but you don't get drawn into the endless stream of thoughts.

Second, recognizing your thoughts is secondary to the main activity you are doing. If you are walking, then your focus is on walking. If you are eating, your focus is on eating. When a thought arises, you notice it. But when there is no thought, you don't waste your energy waiting for the next thought to come. If you are anticipating a thought, you are likely to end up getting lost in thinking instead of being aware of the process.

Third, most thoughts follow a pattern. They are the same. There's nothing new about them. The objective here is not to be aware of all your thoughts, but to build a habit of awareness so you can recognize your common thought patterns and your reactions to them. Most of our habitual thoughts help us in life, anyway, and we don't need to do anything about them. For example, when I reached out for the pair of scissors to open the chocolate bar. We are more concerned with thoughts that trigger emotional reactions.

There are different ways to become more aware of your thoughts. Below are the four activities that I practice. You can use this as a guide, or you can come up with something of your own. Just note that a good activity is something that can:

- Help you break out of your habitual thinking patterns
- Remind you of the difference between your true self and your mind.

1. Use an Alarm

Awareness of your thoughts can be difficult to achieve, especially if you are a beginner. You will need something to constantly remind you to be aware. If there isn't something external to wake you up from your self-criticism habit, you will not remember to be aware of your thoughts. Even if you are not a beginner, it would still be good to use an alarm clock or your phone. I first used an alarm eight years ago and I'm still using it now. The period of time in between when I didn't use the timer was when my life was going downhill and I had depression.

All of us need an external reminder to shake us out of our habitual ways of thinking.

You might be concerned that setting an alarm will be disruptive to your work, but it is meant to be so. If it's not, it won't be effective in changing your mental habits. The last time, when I was working in the office, I used to set an hourly alarm on my phone to remind me to check the quality of my thoughts. It rang when I was focused on my work. It rang when I was talking to my manager. I was annoyed at times, but it was useful. Every time I checked, I was surprised by how noisy and negative my thoughts were. So learn to welcome the alarm; it can be a great spiritual teacher.

To make the sound less intrusive, you can set the timer to the vibrational mode when you are at work or otherwise engaged. Whether you use sound or vibration, make sure it's distinctive, so you don't mix it up with other messages coming in on your phone. In fact, switch off the other message functions so you don't get confused.

Nowadays, I've incorporated the alarm into my work. I do this by using the Pomodoro Technique, a time management technique created by Francesco Cirillo in the late 1980s. The idea is to break down your work into time-blocks and take a short break in between each time-block. After four time-blocks or more, you can schedule a longer break. The key is to be extremely focused on your work during the time-blocks, and let your mind relax regularly during the short breaks. It's important to take breaks when the timer sounds because it will help you re-energize and focus on your next task. During the break, you can do a stretch, go to the restroom, or take a walk. I use the break time to check my thoughts and maintain awareness. I call this "The Mindfulness Break." These breaks are supposed to help you be more productive, but you can use them for spiritual practice, too.

The duration of the blocks and what you do for your breaks are up to you. For the technique to be effective, it is best to set the time-blocks to 45 minutes or less. I set my working time to 27 minutes and breaks to three minutes. I'm not too rigid with the longer breaks, though. I don't set alarms for them. When I get tired after a few time-blocks (usually four to six), I just take a longer break to eat something, read a book, or chat with someone.

You can download a timer app to help you with this technique. Just search for the phrase "Pomodoro Timer" in your app store and choose the app that you like. The one I'm using is called *Brain Focus*. For some of you who like to listen to the sound of the bell, you can search for "Mindfulness Bell." The sound of the bell will remind you to be mindful as you take your break.

2. Single-Tasking

A Russian Proverb says: *If you chase two rabbits, you will not catch either one.* It's the same when it comes to thoughts: *if you follow two streams of thought, you will be aware of none.*

In the book, *The One Thing*, by Gary Keller and Jay Papasan, the authors mention that we can do two things at a time, but we can't focus on two things or more at a time. Let's say you are using a part of your brain to complete a task. When you want to perform another task, you will have to shift your attention from one part of your brain to another part of your brain. Even if you are still doing the first task, the focus won't be on your first task anymore, but on the second task.

Most of us can't put our attention on different parts of our brain at the same time. Shifting from task to task only exhausts our brain power and we end up relying on our habits. When we multitask, we allow the different streams of thoughts inside our head to lead us. Our conscious minds are too tired to question their accuracy. Everything we do becomes automatic and we miss the essence of our thoughts. This allows thoughts to slip between the cracks and take control of our consciousness.

Single-tasking allows you to hear your thoughts clearly.

When we are present and focused on one task, we become naturally more aware of our distracting thoughts. These thoughts are so distinctive; it's like hearing a pin drop in a quiet room. When you do one task mindfully, any thought that takes you away from your presence or intrudes on your activity can be detected easily. This is why mindfulness practitioners often focus only on one task at a time

For example, when you put 100% of your attention on eating your meal and enjoying every bite of the food, any unsupportive thought will be loud and clear. It's easy for us to be aware of it because it has nothing to do with the food we are eating. But if we are eating while using our phones or talking to others at the same time, even if thoughts surface, we might not be able to hear them because there are too many things requiring our attention simultaneously.

Sometimes, it's tough to single-task, especially for

those who are so used to multitasking. The key is to set a clear intention before you begin a task and create an environment that fosters single-tasking. Again, I use the Pomodoro Technique to help me with this. Before I write each morning, I review what I'm going to write. When I press the start button on my Pomodoro app, I know I have to focus on my writing. If any other thoughts arise that take me away from my writing, I make a mental note for later or write it down on a piece of paper. As for my environment, I clear the table and remove any clutter that might cause distractions or that is not related to the task I'm about to do. I'll also close the door to minimize external disturbance.

3. Journaling

Sometimes it's not easy to notice your negative thoughts. You can set an alarm, but you might be still thinking about your work when you take your break. Perhaps you are so engrossed in your work that you ignore or switch off your alarm. There might also be days when you unknowingly let yourself get distracted by your critical thoughts and spend hours reacting to them.

Journaling can be your last line of defense. It will allow you to capture the mistakes you make during the day. It gives you the opportunity to present your thoughts externally and identify negative thought patterns. When you are able to see your thoughts in writing, it can help you avoid identifying with them.

Journaling helps us to look at our thoughts instead of looking from the perspective of our thoughts.

There are a couple of ways to journal. You can do it whenever your mind gets noisy, or you can do it at the end of the day as part of your daily review.

The first way is to use journaling to check the quality of your thoughts at any given moment. We already tried this at the beginning of this chapter. All you need to do is to grab a pen and a piece of paper and write down whatever thoughts come into your mind for two to five minutes using bullet points. After this, you can review the thoughts you've written and identify the beliefs behind them.

This method is good for capturing and distinguishing the different types and forms of self-criticism. Some negative thinking can come in the form of questions. Instead of *You should be ashamed of yourself,* it can also be a rhetorical question such as *Don't you think what you've done is wrong?* Both statements make you feel bad about yourself, even though they are phrased differently.

There are also many different types of criticism. In the book *Freedom from Your Inner Critic* by Jay Earley Ph.D. and Bonnie Weiss, the authors have identified seven specific types of inner critics, including:

- The Perfectionist
- The Inner Controller
- The Taskmaster
- The Underminer
- The Destroyer
- The Guilt Tripper
- The Molder

You can use the naming conventions suggested in this book, or create your own names for your inner critics. Some people even draw their inner critics out in order to separate themselves from their inner critics. Most importantly, knowing about the various forms and types of self-criticism can help you become more aware of them in the future.

4. Evening Review

I prefer to use the second method of journaling, which is to include it as part of my daily review. Every evening after dinner, I do a review of my day. During this time, I reflect on what I've done during the day, including what I did well and how I could improve the results. I'll write everything down and bring the lessons I have learned to the next day.

**We can see our actions,
but we can't see our thoughts and emotions.**

The reason why reflection is so useful is that we are more aware of behaviors than our thoughts and emotions. We can *see* how the actions we took don't serve us, but we can't *see* our thoughts and emotions very well. Some people who are more in tune with their emotions might be able to recognize they are feeling angry and unhappy, but they might not be aware of the negative thoughts that have triggered these feelings.

Our thoughts, emotions, and actions influence one another. If you can't pinpoint your thoughts, pay attention to your emotions and actions instead. Write down how you feel and act during the day. Then, use this to trace back to your underlying thoughts and beliefs. (More on this in Chapter 8.)

The good thing about having a daily review is that when your mind gets noisy, you can tell it to come back later and share with you in the evening. I acknowledge the existence of my inner critic and give it a platform to discuss the issues and concerns with me. In this way, I can focus on the task at hand and not get distracted by my critical thoughts. Also, doing a review daily helps relieve or solve any problems I am facing on a daily basis instead of letting them accumulate and snowball into something unmanageable such as depression.

Again, there are no hard and fast rules about the evening review. Instead of doing it after dinner, you could choose to do it just before bed, right after you brush your teeth. How much to write also depends on you. If you have the time, you can spend 30 minutes or more doing your review. Usually, I spend 5 to 15 minutes and only write down one area of improvement. I find it more effective to work on one area at a time, instead of listing several things that I'm less likely to accomplish.

Chapter 6

Step #2: Disbelieve All Thoughts

"Reducing your forward momentum is the first step to freeing yourself from the beliefs, habits, feelings, and busyness that may be limiting you."

— PETER BREGMAN, 18 MINUTES

When we were children, we possessed the power of doubt. We questioned everything our parents told us. When our parents asked us to do something, we asked them why: *Why do we have to brush our teeth? Why do we have to go to bed early? Why does Dad get to watch the TV and we don't?* We were curious and asked many questions about the people and the world around us.

To most parents, this stage of parenting is rather frustrating because their every response is followed up with yet another question. But what really annoys them is that their children ask questions they cannot answer. As adults, most of the things we do are based on what was passed down by our grandparents or the social norms. We follow these rules because of survival, and because that's what everyone else is doing. We don't question why we do what we do anymore. So when children ask their parents questions about why they have to do certain things, some parents brush them off: *What do you mean, why? Just do what I tell you to do,* or they lie in order to get their children to do what they want: *If you don't behave and sit down and be quiet, the police will come and catch you.*

Not only are children curious, they are very doubtful, too. When you tell them not to do something, some will continue to do it because they simply don't believe you. It's not that children are naughty or disobedient. They don't have the concept of what's right or wrong yet, so they want to test what they can do or cannot do. Children only give up trying when something bad happens to them repeatedly, for example falling off the couch or getting burned by the hot kettle. They need to learn it for themselves before they will start listening to their parents. This is the power of doubt.

Over time, children follow their parents; they stop doubting their thoughts.

However, once we start to listen to our parents and believe what they say, our desire to doubt begins to lessen. Our minds are so comfortable operating on autopilot that we don't question what we do anymore.

Fortunately for us, we haven't lost our ability to doubt, we just don't use it actively. Every time we choose to listen to one subpersonality over another, we are, in essence, doubting. We have so many subpersonalities living in our heads. If we were to believe all their views, we would find ourselves unable to function, survive, and make decisions. Sometimes, even our inner critics get overruled by the other more positive subpersonalities. When your inner critic tells you: *He doesn't even like you. Why would he be interested in you?*, another voice in your head might override it: *What if he feels the same for you? Don't miss out on that opportunity.* Sometimes, you feel unworthy and sometimes you are hopeful, depending on which voice you believe.

Most of us take a passive role in disbelieving. We doubt our thoughts so unintentionally that we don't realize our inner critics can't hurt us if we *choose* not to believe what they say. In this chapter, we will learn how to be more intentional in doubting our thoughts.

Why Disbelieve All of Your Thoughts?

The second step of the Disbelief Process is to disbelieve *all* of the thoughts you are aware of. Yes, all of them. We are not just doubting our negative thoughts; we are doubting all thoughts. As mentioned in the beginning, most thoughts are just our perception of reality – they aren't real. Once you become aware of a thought, the immediate thing to do is remind yourself not to trust it. Here's why you don't have to isolate the bad thoughts from the positive ones:

1. It's difficult to evaluate all your thoughts.

Conventional wisdom will tell you to accentuate the positive and eliminate the negative. But judging a thought and determining whether it's good or bad requires energy. It makes the brain work harder. We have so many thoughts a day. It's tedious and time-consuming for the conscious mind to evaluate each one of them and single out the negative ones.

If you want to develop a new habit or replace an old one, make it easy for your brain to perform the new routine. Otherwise, you might give up when it gets tough and revert to your old habits. Disbelieving all of your thoughts is easier and more straightforward than deciding which thoughts to doubt. It helps cut down the step of judging your thoughts and requires little or no effort from you.

Disbelieving your thoughts
doesn't require you to do anything.

You just need to listen and observe. After you have doubted your thoughts, if you still feel the urge to react, let it be. The habit energy within you is still very strong and it is pushing you to act in a way you are used to. The purpose of this step is not to stop your reaction. It's to open you up to the possibility that your thoughts could be wrong. It will also disrupt the forward momentum of your habits.

When self-criticism arises, even if it's just one short second of disbelief before you react to it out of habit, it's good enough, as there is a little gap between your thoughts and your awareness. You aren't unconsciously controlled and blindly following the instructions of your mind anymore. This will help you see that your mind-made stories aren't true. It also weakens the power of your habits, and you won't feel as rewarded by reacting to your critical thoughts.

2. It's pointless to isolate your thoughts because they are all neutral.

Our thoughts are neither negative nor positive, at first. They are neutral. They only become positive or negative when we judge them so. Statements such as *I'm not good enough, I'm not worthy of love,* and *I don't deserve to be successful* have no impact on us if we don't believe them. On the contrary, believing the so-called "positive" statements *I can do it, I deserve to be loved,* and *I'm going to reach my goals* doesn't necessarily make you happier. They might cause disappointment or suffering when things don't turn out as expected.

Positive thoughts can have a negative outcome you don't desire. We don't know for sure if a thought will have a positive or negative outcome until we act on it. If you are someone who does creative work, you will know that your first idea isn't always your best idea. A seemingly good idea might not have the impact you expect it to have.

Thoughts are suggestions,
and suggestions are not be taken as the truth.

Thoughts represent the different perceptions of your subpersonalities. There is no right or wrong. A neutral thought can also lead to criticism. Sometimes, when I get stuck in my writing, my mind tells me to do some research online. Researching for information is a harmless, neutral action. But if I wasn't alert enough and followed one suggestion after another, I might end up indulging in too much research or watching some random video online, and then get a scolding from my inner critic for not focusing on my work.

Your self-criticism isn't started by your inner critic, it starts way back when one of your subpersonalities gave you a random suggestion. Instead of selecting and disbelieving only the critical thoughts, it's better to doubt all suggestions first and treat all your subpersonalities and thoughts equally.

3. True skepticism doesn't take any position.

When you decide that a thought is positive or negative, you have already failed to disbelieve. True skepticism requires you to be open and suspend all your judgment. When you think something is good, your mind will naturally defend and want more of it. When you think something is bad, your mind will naturally resist it and want less of it. No matter what position you take, you fall into the trap your mind has created for you. You have believed that one thought is better than another.

Once you dismiss a thought as negative, you don't get to see the value it brings.

You can't check the authenticity of a thought when your mind has preconceived assumptions about it. When you disbelieve, you need to remove any beliefs you have about your thoughts. It's like double-checking your work. You don't check your work with the assumption that you are correct. You check your work as though you are doing something new for the first time.

Nelly, from the story earlier on, said that she checks her work but she still makes careless mistakes. I was curious about this, and so I asked her one day, "How do you check your work?"

She replied that she uses the calculator to check her work. Finally, I understood why she wasn't able to notice her mistakes. She had assumed that her working and steps were correct and so only the calculation could be wrong. But checking the calculation is pointless if the working is wrong in the first place. She had neglected to check her answers as though she was working on the questions for the first time, and this allowed mistakes to go unnoticed.

Disbelieving doesn't mean that you don't take any action. You don't need to know whether your thoughts are positive or not in order to act on them. It's about testing them out for yourself and being your own investigator. You don't have to follow or react to your thoughts, but this doesn't mean you can't take suggestions, either. It's unlike when you judge your thoughts; you are already limiting your choices right at the start.

How to Separate Fact from Fiction

For beginners, I know how difficult it is to disbelieve your thoughts, especially the critical ones. We often question what other people tell us, but we seldom question what our inner critics have to say. The criticisms sound so real that you can't help but to believe them. When you are first starting out on this step in the process, it is good to ask the question: *Is this thought true?*

Asking the question, "Is this true?", opens you to the possibility that your thoughts can be false.

You don't even have to believe your self-criticism is false. You just need to hold on to the possibility that it *might* be false. Doing this will already help you a lot in the Disbelief Process.

Our minds are extremely good at telling stories. This is how we communicate and learn from each other. But telling yourself stories doesn't create the inner peace you desire. Be it a happy or sad story, the stories your mind tells you are often exaggerated and untrue.

Below is a list of common words our inner critics use to make us feel unworthy. The list is not meant to be exhaustive, but it can give you a good start in learning how to separate the truth from fiction. Just be careful not to get into a logical, cognitive debate with your subconscious. Remember, it doesn't listen to reason. It's not about changing your beliefs, either. It's about not believing your beliefs. Just know that what your mind says isn't always the truth.

1. I am _____ .

Fill in the blank with: a bad parent, a pushover, a nobody, a loser, lazy, stupid, too sensitive, too quiet....

Perhaps the two most powerful words in the English language are: "I am." We use these two words to describe ourselves and build our identity. The words that follow not only determine how we view ourselves, they also have a huge impact on how we live, behave, think, and feel.

When we constantly use positive statements such as: *I am kind, I am compassionate,* and *I am a good person,* we are more likely to feel good about ourselves and the people around us. However, if we keep using negative statements such as: *I am boring, I am a failure,* and *I am unlovable,* we end up having low self-esteem, feeling lonely, and thinking other people are against us.

We often use the words "I am" even when the situation has nothing to do with us. For example, when someone tells us the food we cooked tastes salty, we think they are implying that we are bad cooks. When our relationship with someone doesn't work out, we are quick to assume we are unlovable or unworthy. Even if we have made mistakes in the relationship, it just means that we have made mistakes. It has nothing to do with our self-worth. *I made mistakes in my relationship* is not to be confused with *I am a mistake.* The former focuses on the mistakes, while the latter focuses on you as a person. Taking anything personal is a sure way to upset yourself.

The sun doesn't say "I am the sun,"
it simply is the sun.
You don't have to describe yourself; just be you.

The problem with using the words "I am" is that it simply doesn't represent who we are at the moment. Whenever we used the words "I am," our subconscious minds pull out any stories from the past that might support the statement we have just made. If you think you are a failure, your mind will dig out all those times when you failed and magnify the intensity of your current failure. Your past defeats are not a good representation of who you are right now. So it's best is to let go of any judgment you have about yourself and just be.

2. I am not _____ enough.

Fill in the blank with: good, unique, special, perfect, deserving, successful, beautiful, hardworking....

Unlike the words "I am," which emphasize our negative traits, the words "not enough" focus on our lack of positive traits. Whenever we use the words "not enough," we are comparing ourselves to an ideal self-image, our unrealistic expectations, or other people. It makes us feel unfulfilled.

I am not good enough is one of the most common lies we tell ourselves. Most of us don't have a standard for "good enough" to begin with. If you say you are not good enough, what do you need to achieve to feel good enough? A million dollars? Approval from all your friends and family? Everyone to like you?

If we don't have a measure for our self-worth, how can we reach our goals, including the goal of having a fulfilling life? We need to know where we are heading before we can determine that we have arrived. Right? Without knowing what "enough" is for you, you will just be criticizing yourself for nothing. So whenever you feel that you are lacking in some way ask yourself:

- What is my definition of "enough"?
- When will it be enough for me?
- Will I truly feel "good enough" when I get what I define as enough?
- Is it even realistic and attainable?

Those of us who have clear standards about what "good enough" means might also suffer from high self-expectations. We set unrealistic goals for ourselves that are impossible to achieve or we pit ourselves against people who are much more successful than we are. Even when we are on our way to achieving our goals, we get frustrated and feel that we aren't reaching them fast enough because we constantly judge ourselves against something or someone we *believe* is better than us.

The ego has the habit of wanting more.
It can never be satisfied.

Our minds have an insatiable hunger that keeps us wanting more. Whenever we attain what we desire, the mind gives us a new challenge to pursue. When we have someone who loves us, we desire more out of the relationship. There will always be a next goal or more things we want to get. Our minds make us believe that we can only feel good enough when we achieve our goals or change ourselves.

But the truth is "enough" will never be enough when we keep chasing after the next big thing. "Enough" can only be felt when we stop and appreciate what we have and who we are in the present. It isn't something we can get externally; it's something that we already possess internally. Only we can make ourselves feel loved, adequate, and good enough in every given moment.

3. I should (or shouldn't) have _____ .

Fill in the blank with: (for "should have") exercised, been more careful, spent more time on my project, known better, (for "shouldn't have") watched the TV, eaten the snacks, been so naive, wasted my time....

Anytime we use the word "should" or "shouldn't," we are judging our behaviors and limiting ourselves based on what we *think* is good for us or what is acceptable by our society. We are basically telling ourselves that what we have done or haven't done is wrong. But unlike the words "I am," we use the words "should" and "shouldn't" to criticize our actions and enforce our lack of self-worth and identity. People who believe in using criticism to motivate and discipline themselves use these two words frequently to punish themselves for their perceived mistakes.

However, using these two words often leads to the same self-judgment and negative emotions; for example, when we tell ourselves we should have known better. We usually also interpret that we are dumb, naive, or at fault for not knowing better and we feel bad about it. Furthermore, whenever we say we *should* do something, we are reinforcing the idea that we are *not* doing it. So how motivating can this be?

I should have exercised. I should have stayed in my job. I should have spent more time with my kids. How many self-imposed judgments such as these are actually valid? So what if you didn't exercise today. Did it have any impact on your health? What if you had stayed in your job? Can you predict with certainty that your life would have been better? And if you had been more aware previously, would you have spent more time with your kids?

Not only do our inner critics love to evaluate our actions, they love to exaggerate the impact our actions have on us. Missing a day of your exercise schedule doesn't necessarily affect your health. But we fabricate stories in our heads, telling ourselves how lazy we are or how we might skip other sessions, too, and how it will eventually affect our health. The same goes for the other two examples; we can't be sure what would have happened instead if we had stayed in our jobs or spent more time with our kids. But our minds use these invalidated stories to blame us for what we have done or not done.

The truth is you can't change your past,
and you don't know what the future brings.

The word "should" takes us out of the present moment and creates unnecessary suffering. Wishing something would be different doesn't help change it. If you have done something wrong, you can't undo it no matter how much "should" you use. You can only make amendments in the present. When we use the word "should," we are not accepting reality and taking responsibility for what we have or have not done. We are just running away from the truth.

4. I am always (or will never) _____ .

Fill in the blank with: (for "am always") wrong, late, forgetful, indecisive, (for "will never") be successful, find someone who loves me, get this right, have the relationship I want....

Two words that I catch myself using frequently are "always" and "never." We often use them and not just with ourselves, but also with other people who are close to us, such as our partner, parents, and kids. Some examples might be: *You never put things back in their original place, You never do the laundry,* and *You always make the same mistakes.* But are our accusations towards others and ourselves valid?

The mind uses these two words to exaggerate and create drama: "always" and "never."

Whenever I was late, my inner critic would make statements such as: *You are always late. You should have left home earlier."*

One day, I reflected on this and realized: *Hey, I'm not always late. Yes, I might be late one out of ten times, but I am usually early or on time most of the time. Why did my inner critic say I'm always late? What a false accusation!*

Are you always as bad as what your inner critic exaggerates you to be? Many times, you're not. When you tell yourself: *I always get things wrong,"* do you really get it wrong *every single* time? If not, how can you conclude that you are always incorrect? Even if you do make mistakes frequently but there's one time you are correct, then you can't say that you make mistakes *all* the time. It's just not true. The word "never" works the same way. When we say we are never happy or successful, it excludes all the times we are perfectly fine and successful.

It's easier to identify our mistakes and beat ourselves up than to recognize and remember the successes we have had along the way. The mind is so eager to conclude we are bad that it magnifies our negative behaviors and finds evidence from the past to support the accusation. But the words "always" and "never" are like death sentences. Our minds are so fixed on who we are in a negative way that we never have a chance to improve our lives.

If the mind's role is to spot problems and exaggerate them, then our role is to uncover the exaggerations and not believe them.

5. No one (or everyone) _____ .

Fill in the blank with: (for "no one") loves me, cares about me, understands me, supports what I do (for "everyone") hates me, finds me boring, is better than me, thinks I'm ugly….

Unlike the other criticisms, this one is not about how you view yourself; it's about how you *think* other people view you. But similar to the words "always" and "never," we use the words "no one," "nobody," and "everyone" for exaggeration purposes.

One of the most hurtful lies my inner critic used to tell me was: *No one loves you.* I used to believe this lie because I felt neglected by my parents and my classmates. But did I actually ask everyone if they love me or not? Of course not. I didn't even validate this belief with my parents but just assumed they didn't love me based on my misinterpretations as a kid.

How can we conclude that no one loves us when we haven't confirmed it with everyone?

When we use words like "no one," we use it for the dramatic effect. We can't say "no one" unless we have checked it with everyone to prove our case. When someone doesn't like us, it doesn't mean that everyone else doesn't like us. But since it is impossible to get everyone's opinion about us, this opinion can never be verified. You can list the people who don't like you, but you can't say that everyone doesn't like you. Using such exaggerated words will only make you feel more lonely, disconnected, and separated from the world.

Not everyone will love and understand you, but that's okay because there are many others who do. I know that not everyone will like my books, and not everyone will agree with what I have written. But that doesn't imply that no one likes my books. Everyone has their own preference and beliefs, and I'm writing for those who like my writing style.

Lastly, the words, "no one" can only be true if we

include ourselves. So whenever you think that no one loves, cares about, or understands you, it's a cue that you need to dedicate more time and attention to loving yourself.

Mastering Disbelief

There are two parts to perception. One is the sensory perception. This is when you receive information from your five senses. The other is the interpretation of the information – the meanings and stories you give to the information you receive. Disbelieving is about doubting the latter.

After you have questioned your thoughts for some time, you will realize there is no need to question them anymore. You have already established a gap between the thought and you, the perceiver. Whenever a thought arises, just maintain this gap and not get drawn into the convincing stories your mind has crafted. There's no need to convince your mind of the truth.

To master disbelief, you need to know that words are limiting. Your mind will want to make something out of the situation. It wants polarities so the story will be interesting. But the adjectives we use to describe ourselves and our circumstances are influenced by our personal feelings and preferences. They don't represent the truth.

We know the truth can hardly be expressed in words.

Is the cup half empty or half full? No matter how you judge it or what perspective you take, it doesn't take away the essence of what the cup is. It only affects your perception of reality. If you think the cup is half empty, then this becomes true for you. If you think the cup is half full, then this will be your reality. Both are "right" only within the realm of your mind. The cup is still the cup with some water in it. The truth doesn't change because of your perception of what the cup is. The essence of who you are doesn't change because of the way you describe yourself.

Perceiving what *is* will help you stay grounded. It will also help you understand the truth in every situation. When you are in a neutral state and perceive without believing the judgment your mind makes, you are in disbelief mode and you can see the wisdom that is right in front of you.

Chapter 7

Step #3: Notice Your Reaction

> *"People's minds are changed through observation and not through argument."*
>
> — WILL ROGERS

My body was shaking uncontrollably and there was nothing I could do about it. I was eight and I had epilepsy. The first time I had a seizure, I was mostly unconscious. The only recollection I have is that when I opened my eyes briefly at the A&E (Accident and Emergency) department in the hospital, my dad was carrying me and looking for a doctor. But I don't remember what happened next or afterwards. When I woke up, I was already in the hospital ward.

The second time I had a seizure (which is also the last time, thankfully), I had it at home when I was nine. I will never forget the experience. Unlike the first seizure, I was more conscious this time. Instead of waking up in the morning quietly, like I usually do, I woke up with my limbs jerking involuntarily. My body became tense, convulsed, and shook violently. My teeth were clenched and foam was coming out of my mouth. I wanted to stop the movements of my body, but my brain wouldn't listen. I wanted to call for help, but I couldn't. I had no control over my body and all I could do was surrender and watch the seizure unfold.

My parents and my aunt were in the room and they were in a panic: *What should we do? Do we have to put something in his mouth so he doesn't bite his tongue? What should we put in his mouth? A metal spoon? A towel?* They decided to shove a metal spoon between my clenched teeth. (By the way, most experts advise not to put anything inside the mouth of a person who is having a seizure because it can cause injury.)

The atmosphere in the room was confusing and chaotic. But somehow, I was rather detached from it. Perhaps I didn't have control over my body and the situation. It felt as though I was watching a movie. Even though I was aware of what was happening, I felt more like an observer than a participant. My body was shaking but I felt peaceful inside. Eventually, the seizure stopped and I went back to sleep a bit more. I woke up later feeling as though nothing had happened.

When you have no control over something, the best you can do is to surrender and observe.

The reason why I share this story is to illustrate that we don't have as much control in life as we think. We can't control our subconscious minds; we can only influence them. Even after we are aware of our thoughts and disbelieve them, sometimes we can't stop the momentum because the habit energy is too strong. We might have understood from a conceptual level that our thoughts are untrue, but at the subconscious level we might still be holding onto our negative self-beliefs and emotional wounds. When our inner critics tell us that we aren't good enough, we might still feel sad, uneasy, or want to run away.

Like a seizure, these feelings will go away eventually. Instead of fighting the energy, the best you can do is surrender and observe. You don't have to suppress your feelings. They will provide you with information you can work with later on. The key is to collect the information through mindful observation and not get carried away by your habits and emotions.

How to Notice Your Reactions

The third step of the Disbelief Process is to notice your reactions. After you have completed the first two steps of the process, the next step is to immediately anchor yourself to something physical. Anchoring helps you to stay present and widen the awareness you have established in the first two steps. It prevents you from getting drawn into the mental stories, images, and emotions created by the mind and helps you to see and feel your reactions from a third-person point of view.

Anchoring to something physical separates you from the gushing streams of thoughts and emotions.

Imagine you are carried away by the strong currents of a river. At first, you are likely to grab onto anything you can find to stop yourself from drifting further downstream or going under and drowning. The same applies to our thoughts and emotions. The strong emotions we experience can pull us in a direction we don't want to go. One thought leads to another, and we can get lost in our thoughts pretty quickly. If we don't anchor ourselves to something physical, we can't even observe our reactions because we are so deep in our suffering and habits. We won't be detached enough to pick up the valuable information our reactions can give us.

There are many things you can use to anchor your focus. As long as it is something that utilizes your sense perception and takes your attention away from the mind, it's most likely to work. For example, you can use objects in your physical environment, such as the chair you are sitting on, the floor you are standing on, or the wall in front of you. You can also focus your attention on a part of your body, such as your hands or feet. If not, you can use sounds, such as the ticking of a clock or a mindfulness bell to help you get centered.

By far, the most commonly used anchor is the breath. It's always accessible, so you don't have to waste time finding your anchor when you are experiencing strong emotions. Just focus on your breath immediately. The only time when it's not quite so suitable to use your breath as an anchor is when you have a panic attack. When I had panic attacks, I couldn't focus on my breath because I was hyperventilating. The more I focused on it, the more I worried that something bad was going to happen to me.

After you have anchored your attention to something, the next action will be to simply watch what happens next. Observe how your body reacts to the situation.

- Do you feel tightness in your chest?
- Is your heart racing?
- Do you find it difficult to breathe deeply?
- Do you feel pain in your stomach?
- Is your face blushing or warm?
- Do you feel the urge to do something or run away?

More importantly, don't describe what you feel in words or name your emotions just yet. Pay attention to exactly how your body feels and your bodily sensations. Notice the thoughts your mind comes up with, but don't follow the stream of thoughts. Just take note of them. Let them surface, acknowledge their existence, and let them go gently. Even if your habit energy is extremely powerful and you have the compulsion to react, it's okay to go with the flow. You are reacting to the situation with awareness now, instead of behaving mindlessly. Your purpose in performing this habit is to collect information. So as long as you stay alert, it's fine.

After the waves of emotions and thoughts have subsided, you can jot down the details you have noticed on a piece of paper. The more often you are aware of your reactions, the better you will become at catching your reaction the next time. When I had depression, I could feel the left side of my head beating vigorously like a heartbeat – it was always on the left side. The right side of my brain had no such reaction. After recovering from depression, I used this physical information as an indication that I might be overthinking and ruminating. So now whenever I feel the left side of my head reacting in this way, I know it's time to relax and let go of the problem I'm trying to solve.

The information you collect can also help you identify your most frequently used reactions. Below are some of the things you might have noticed.

Ruminate

In rumination, most of the actions take place in the head. You probably notice that your mind is more active than usual and flooded with repetitive thoughts. You are focusing your attention internally in order to solve a problem in your head, so you aren't that aware of your physical surrounding. You might also feel some stiffness around the chest area when you are stuck and can't find a solution to a problem.

Resign

In resignation, check to see whether there's any uncomfortable sensation in your body. When you feel like you are not good enough, you will probably notice coldness around the chest area. There might be more reactions around your face area, especially around your eyes and nose when you are welled up with emotions. Your body might also turn inwards as though you are trying to hug and protect your broken heart.

Escape

Escape is probably the hardest to identify of these four because there is a tendency to numb your emotions and ignore your thoughts. The best way to identify which of these four you are manifesting is through observing your activities. One way to tell is to check whether you are doing an activity intentionally or not. Escape behaviors are usually spontaneous and unintentional, but note that not all spontaneous activities are forms of reactive escape. Another way to tell is to be aware of how happy you are after doing an activity. If you keep doing something and you don't enjoy it or you feel indifferent, then most likely it's a form of escape.

Fight

When you fight your inner critic, there will be a lot of activity in both the mind and the body. A part of your mind keeps looping the same thoughts to defend and protect its position. Unlike resignation, though, you will feel more energy to take action and more heat in your body. You might find yourself breathing heavily from anger and direct your anger inwards at yourself or outwards to other people when you feel they threaten your identity.

Finding the Triggers

Even though the third step of the Disbelief Process is to notice your reaction, for most beginners in mindfulness this might be the first step. Some thoughts come so fast and are so subtle that we are not aware of them until we react to them. Feelings and habits are much easier to recognize. We can usually tell when we are in a bad mood because of how it affects our energy level, and we can recognize our bad habits through observing our repeated behaviors.

If you are aware of an emotion or reaction, start by using it as the starting point to uncover the thoughts or beliefs that might have triggered the emotion. Work backward: start from step #3 and go back to steps #1 and

#2. For example, if you catch yourself surfing the Internet mindlessly, ask yourself: *What am I supposed to be doing right now? What thoughts triggered me to surf the Internet with no useful purpose?* Perhaps you had work to do, but you were stuck, so you distracted yourself with the Internet. Maybe you had nothing to do and were feeling bored, so you went online to find something to keep your mind occupied.

Basically, there are two questions to ask yourself when you realize you are reacting:

1. What self-criticism am I reacting to?
2. What are the cues that trigger self-criticism in me?

Identifying Self-Criticism

It's difficult to identify the self-criticism when you have missed it the first time. Plus, some thoughts are nonverbal, like the thought I had about grabbing the scissors. It's almost impossible to notice them. The key objective here is not about finding the exact wording for your critical thought. It's about understanding the main area in which your inner critic attacks you or the general beliefs you have about yourself. Questions you can ask include:

- What critical thoughts cause me to react in an undesirable manner?
- Does the inner critic attack my work, relationships, personality, appearance, or self-worth, in general?
- What do I believe about myself that might have caused me to react in such a way?

The inner critic usually picks one or two main areas to criticize. In people who often doubt or overanalyze their relationships, the focus of the inner critic might be mainly on how bad their relationships with others are. So let's say they didn't get a promotion at work. Their inner critic doesn't attack them for their lack of performance at work. Instead, their inner critic attacks them in the area of relationship. For example, *Your manager doesn't like you*, or *You didn't get promoted because you don't get along with your colleagues*.

To test whether a thought causes you to react or not, say the statement to yourself. Suppose you tell yourself: *No one loves me*. If this makes you feel sad, or you feel bodily sensations, then subconsciously you still believe it to be true. So this thought is most likely the one that causes you to react.

You can also ask different questions for each of your

reactions to help you identify the self-criticism better; for example:

Ruminate: What problem am I trying to solve?

The problem you are ruminating about will give you clues to the criticism you have a hard time accepting. It tells you what you wish to be different. For example, when you keep analyzing text messages, emails, or the body language of others, it shows you are not confident in your relationships with others. This is likely to be the area in which your inner critic is frequently harsh with you.

Resign: What beliefs make me feel unworthy?

For someone who catches themselves filled with self-loathing or self-pitying all the time, it would be good to examine the underlying beliefs they have about themselves. Being aware of your self-perceptions can help you figure out what thoughts bring about the negative feelings. Ask yourself: *What makes me feel ashamed? Is there something I dislike about myself? What belief do I have that makes me hate myself?*

Escape: What am I supposed to do in the first place?

The thing you are running away from is most likely to be the thing you are afraid of being criticized for. To uncover the motivation behind your reactions, you can also ask yourself why you feel compelled to run away. Do you escape from work because you don't want to affirm your incompetence? Do you run away from commitment because you think you are undeserving?

Fight: What thoughts am I trying to resist?

The thing you are actively trying to defend is the thought you are trying to resist. For example, if you are offended or defensive when someone criticizes your work, it is obvious that your self-worth is somewhat linked to your work. You believe that when your work is bad, it means you are bad.

Identifying the Cues that Trigger Self-Criticism

For some of us, it's easier to identify the cues that trigger self-criticism than the criticism itself. If this is the case for you, start with the cues first and figure out the self-criticism later.

Let's say you catch yourself binge eating on some snacks and don't recall what happened that caused you to binge. Trace back to a time you can recall. What happened at that time? What were you doing? Suppose you remember you were surfing social media on your mobile phone prior to binge eating – try to recall the last thing you did. Then, use it to infer the thoughts that might have caused you to react. Perhaps you saw a friend's profile on social media. She is successful and beautiful, and this made you feel a little inferior. Maybe no one likes the posts you put up on social media and you feel disappointed.

Of course, your impression might be totally inaccurate. So instead of concluding it is true, test it out. Go back to your friend's profile on social media and look at it again. How does it make you feel? Observe any thoughts or body sensations that you might have. Does it make you want to escape and eat something? Don't try to filter or suppress your reactions. Just stay conscious and try to notice them.

Sometimes, it's also difficult to pinpoint your exact triggers or critical thoughts immediately. You might have to gather and record the cues for a period of time before you can see the pattern. In Charles Duhigg's book, *The Power of Habits,* he suggests five main categories to record the cues. I've rearranged them to form the acronym "PETAL":

- People
- Emotional state
- Time
- Action
- Location

People

This refers to the people around us or with us. Are we alone? Is there anyone else near us when we have the urge to criticize ourselves?

Emotional State

This refers to our feelings and thoughts just before our negative self-talk occurred. Are we feeling lonely? Unloved? Or perhaps judged?

Time

What time is the inner critic triggered? Be as exact as possible; for example, 4:17 p.m.

Action

What are we doing right before we talk negatively to

ourselves? It doesn't have to be something important. It could be reading an email or staring out the window.

Location

Where are you when you have the negative thought? Be specific with the location. Instead, of writing down "at home," write down which room you were in and which part of the room.

Here's a simplified example of how this works. Let's say you recorded the following information when you realized you were criticizing yourself:

Trigger 1

1. People: With my friends.
2. Emotional state: Feel left out.
3. Time: 12:15 p.m.
4. Action: Listening to my friends having a great conversation over lunch.
5. Location: Happy Deli.

Trigger 2

1. People: By myself in my work cubicle, but there are other colleagues in the office.
2. Emotional state: Feel left out.
3. Time: 7:07 p.m.
4. Action: Overheard that my colleagues are having dinner together.
5. Location: In my office cubicle.

Trigger 3

1. People: With other participants.
2. Emotional state: Feel left out.
3. Time: 8:12 p.m.
4. Action: Standing in a corner eating alone.
5. Location: At a networking event near my office.

After a week or two, you will likely start to see a pattern. Sometimes, it might be a single cue that triggers your habit. Other times, it could be a combination of two or more cues.

From the example above, you can tell that whenever you feel left out, your inner critic attacks you and makes you feel unloved. We can also infer that your triggers mostly involve other people and social settings. You might find that whenever you are alone at home doing your own stuff, your negative self-talk is never triggered. However, when it's time to interact with others, you feel that no one loves you.

Recording this information helps. It's a systematic way of identifying your cues. But if you are a highly intuitive person, you might be able to see the cues and patterns from your past experience without even having to jot down the information. So do what's easiest for you. If you are totally clueless as to what your triggers might be, you can also ask your friends and family for help. They might notice, from a third-person perspective, something you have missed.

Chapter 8

Step #4: Identify the Message

> *"Criticism should not be querulous and wasting, all knife and root-puller, but guiding, instructive, inspiring."*
>
> — RALPH WALDON EMERSON

I immediately regretted asking my friend, Kyle, to return the dollar he owed me. Upon hearing my request, Kyle took out all the loose change he had and picked the smallest coin denominations he could find to make up one dollar. I could tell he was annoyed that I had made this request, especially while we were having lunch in the middle of our vacation in the United States.

But did I really care about getting back the dollar? Of course not. What actually led to this incident was constant nagging from my inner critic and the pressure of taking good photos for my friends.

Four years ago, there were four of us on this trip. Brandon, the official photographer of our group, was in charge of taking the photos. He had brought all his camera equipment with him and taken amazing photos for the group. However, someone had to take photos for him and I was tasked with this job. I didn't mind taking the photos for Brandon, but I felt stressed about possibly not living up to his expectations. Furthermore, my hands tend to get shaky when I'm taking photos. When I'm nervous, they become even more unsteady. I wished my other two friends would help take Brandon's photo, too, but somehow the group perceived me as the next best photographer in the group. So I ended up taking most of Brandon's photos.

On the outside, it appeared that I was feeling stressed. But on the inside, there was something else brewing. For the whole trip, my inner critic kept harping at me to not to be a pushover: *If you don't want to take the photos, tell them so. Don't let other people take advantage of you. Don't be such a pushover!* This wasn't something new to me. Back at home, my inner critic often attacks me for being weak and not standing up for myself. It sounds just like my protective dad, who keeps insisting that we should fight back when other people bully us. But I often ignore this voice.

Whenever I'm in groups, I have a tendency to accommodate others because I value peace and harmony. I don't see being accommodating in the same way as being bullied. If something isn't important to me, it doesn't have to be done my way. However, the nagging voice in my head gets to me sometimes. I don't enjoy being called a pushover. It implies that I'm weak. Sometimes, I defend myself and resist this hurtful accusation. Other days, I end up doing something silly just to prove that I'm not a pushover – and asking Kyle to return my dollar was one of those days.

The night before, I had been contemplating whether I should ask him to give me back the dollar. One part of me was thinking: *It's just a dollar. Why make a big fuss over it?* Then, the other part of me argued: *No, it's not just about the dollar. It's about standing up for yourself. It's your right to ask for what other people owe you. Why can't you do it? Why do you feel embarrassed when you ask for something that belongs to you?* So to prove to my inner critic that I'm not a pushover, I asked Kyle to give me back the dollar I had loaned him.

Just like our parents, the inner critic might mean well but it's horrible at relating its message.

The truth be told, I believe that what the inner critic said made some sense. At the time, I wasn't good at setting boundaries. I didn't often voice my opinions when I needed to. For example, if I was feeling tired, I wouldn't tell my friends that I needed to go home. I would stay until everyone else was tired and wanted to leave. If someone complained, I would sit there and listen even though I didn't enjoy it. I felt a need to prove myself because deep down inside I agreed with my inner critic. I believed I was weak and needed to stand up for myself.

Furthermore, why should anyone feel ashamed of asking for their money back? Is it because the amount was only one dollar and I didn't want to be perceived as someone who is stingy? Am I overly concerned with how others see me?

Our inner critics often bring us important messages that deserve to be explored further. But perhaps the tone in which the message is delivered, the timing, and the context aren't always the most appropriate. Setting boundaries can help me communicate my values to others and improve my relationships. However, I don't need to be called a pushover in order to do it. I also could have settled the one dollar debt at the end of the day, like we usually do, instead of asking for it back in the middle of lunch. It was simply done in the wrong context at the wrong time.

This chapter is about extracting value from our inner critics. It's about identifying the message despite the poor delivery. If we explore the messages our inner critics bring us, they can actually give us great insights into our habits and lives.

How to Get to the Core of the Message

The fourth step in the Disbelief Process is to identify the message. After you notice how you react to your thoughts, some of you might get the message that your inner critic is trying to convey straightaway. But usually it takes a while for the insight to surface.

To have a deeper understanding of the message that your inner critic brings, it's good to create a space and time for regular reflection. As mentioned in Chapter 5, I like to do my review in the evening. I don't just use this time to review the thoughts I had during the day, I also use it to uncover insights. Reflection is a part of my daily routine.

There are different ways to reflect. You can do it with another person through dialogue. You can make it part of your meditative routine. Some people reflect the best when they exercise. I prefer self-inquiry and writing my answers down. Regardless of what method you choose, below are three questions that you can use to help you identify the core message.

1. What is my inner critic trying to protect me from?

All of your subpersonalities, including your inner critic, have a role to play. The inner critic is hard on you for a reason. It won't criticize you unless there is something it needs to protect you from. Whether the thing it is defending you from is justifiable or not, that's another story. Just like our parents, the inner critic safeguards us from harm based on what they believe is dangerous to us. What appears to be harmful to our parents and the inner critic might not necessarily cause us harm. Even if it does, it doesn't mean it's bad for us.

Our inner critic resembles our parents.

You might find that the inner critic's tone, language, or the things it attacks you for are similar to your parents. The inner critic is a subpersonality our minds have created to take over the disciplinary role from our parents. It emulates the voices of our parents and its job is to protect us from danger. Most of our self-criticism is based on beliefs we learned from our childhood, either directly or indirectly from our parents and other people around us. The inner critic is part of our protection mechanism. Our job is to get to the core of the message and understand its intention. *What is it trying to keep us safe from? Is this protection really necessary? Has the inner critic exaggerated the possible consequences in order to get us to do or not do something?*

The key is not to take anything you hear from the inner critic seriously. For example, when my inner critic called me a pushover, the intention wasn't to make me feel bad about myself. It was to protect me from being taken advantage of by others. When your inner critic tells you to exercise and not be so lazy or it reprimands you for eating unhealthy food, it is showing it cares about your health. When your inner critic doubts your capability to succeed and warns you about being too hopeful, it is afraid that you will fail and it doesn't want you to be disappointed. When your inner critic says you don't look good in your dress or shirt, it is afraid you will be judged negatively by others for how you look.

You might not believe that your inner critic is up to anything good and that's okay. It doesn't even matter what the real intention of your inner critic is, use it for your own growth. When my inner critic called me a pushover, I could have chosen to feel bad about myself or I could have extracted lessons that could be applied to my life. It's my choice and I use the inner critic to remind me of the importance of enforcing my boundaries and my positions with other people. Instead of taking criticism personally, I try to extract value from it.

2. Does my past have anything to do with self-criticism?

A good way to identify the message is to check whether there were similar events in your childhood, at home or at school. If your inner critic constantly makes you feel inferior to other people, check to see if there were any major incidents in which you were rejected by your parents or your peers.

- Did you try to please your parents but they give you a cold response?
- Did your parents often compare you to your siblings or other kids?
- Were you teased or humiliated by other children in school?

- Did they make fun of how you look or act?

Check if there is any connection with the past. Ask yourself: *Are my self-criticism habits caused by my previous conditioning or events from the past? Would I still criticize myself the same way if these events had not occurred? What issues from the past have I not resolved yet?*

Self-criticism continues because issues from the past have not been resolved yet.

If you want to significantly reduce the noises in your head, let go of your past. You need to go back to your past and correct the misinterpretations you had as a child and the inaccurate beliefs you developed when you were young. Understand that when you were a child, you might have given the wrong meanings to certain events; realize that these beliefs don't apply to you in the present.

Identifying the message is one way to face the core problem up front and learn how to deal with your pain. Sometimes, it's not easy to forgive the people who hurt you and let go of an incident, especially if you experienced something traumatic such as abuse or bullying. However, if you don't allow yourself to feel your pain, the inner critic will keep bringing it up until you feel it completely and release it from your system. It's just like when our parents keep nagging us to do something and we refused to listen. They will not stop until we have gotten the message and acknowledged what they are saying.

3. What can be improved or changed?

Apart from helping us resolve our past issues, the inner critic can tell us what needs to be improved. If our inner critics are always criticizing us for the same mistakes, perhaps it's time to change our methods of doing things or get help from someone else. It would be better than denying our mistakes and pretending we are right.

The inner critic has the potential to be our inner coach. However, similar to some of our parents, it believes that being harsh will help us change. But more often than not, criticism doesn't work.

Criticism can be constructive if you change the focus.

Criticism focuses on the problem, but this won't give you the solution. Convince your inner critic to focus on solutions instead. Whenever your inner critic tells you what you should or shouldn't do, ask it to tell you what you could do instead. Replace "I should have" with "I could have." So, for example, if your inner critic tells you that you shouldn't have wasted your time on random TV shows, ask it for alternatives: *What can I do instead? Read a book? Go to another room instead of picking up the remote control for the TV?*

Also, look for examples or times when something turned out positive and learn from these experiences: *Were there days when you were focused on your work and had a clear direction on what to do next? Are there times when you have successfully resisted the temptation of watching the TV? How were they different? What did you do on the days that resulted in a different outcome?*

Criticism focuses on the past and there's nothing you can do to change the past. Get your inner critic to tell you what you can improve and change in the future instead. It's more empowering this way because it gives you the opportunity to learn from your mistakes and grow.

Every evening during my review, I get my inner critic to identify what I have done well during the day so I can continue with these actions in the future. Then, I ask it to tell me what I didn't do well and suggest how I can improve. I always start with the words, "I could have..." and let my inner critic complete the sentence. In this way, I always receive constructive criticism. You might not be able to stop your self-criticism totally, but you can always create an environment and a process to facilitate constructive criticism.

Encouraging Your Inner Critic to Be Compassionate

If you want your inner critic to be compassionate towards you, be compassionate towards your inner critic. Respect it for doing its job and not fight with it. When you fight with the inner critic, not only do you waste your energy, you are giving your control away to your inner critic. You are allowing it to affect your mood.

You have the power to make the final decision and determine what information to use. There's no need to defend yourself when someone brings you an opinion that you are not going to use. Instead, thank your inner critic for delivering the message. This applies to all your other subpersonalities, too.

Unlike the other subpersonalities, though, your inner critic usually delivers the message in a tone that we find hard to accept. So, how do you change the tone of your inner critic?

1. Make your boundaries and position clear to your inner critic.

The first thing you can do is let your inner critic know you don't appreciate the way it criticizes you. Let it know it can't talk down to you. Even though your inner critic might be trying to protect you from harm, let it know that talking down to you doesn't help. It only makes things worse.

You can walk away from a person who is nasty, but you can't walk away from your own mind.

When someone attacks you, there is no need to remain seated and allow the attack. You leave. But what if the someone is your own mind? When your inner critic attacks you, do not respond. Even though you can't physically walk away from your mind, you can choose not to give it any attention. This is as good as walking away.

You can make your stand clearly to your inner critic: *I want to work with you. I know you care, but I don't like the way you talk to me. If you want to use this tone, I'm not going to sit here and listen to it. If you want to say something, please say it nicely. Otherwise, please don't speak at all. I am able to listen better when you are kind.*

Your inner critic will have no choice but to change its

tone towards you because it wants your attention. It wants its voice to be heard. You can make your stand either by telling your inner critic in a firm yet compassionate way, or you can write a letter to your inner critic. The key thing is to be firm. Don't pay attention to your inner critic until it changes the way it treats you.

2. Ask your inner critic to suggest, rather than tell.

Your subpersonalities can't tell you what to do. They can only give you suggestions. The only time they are able to tell you what to do is when you forget about the space between the mind and your spiritual self. You forget there is an observer behind all the mental noise, and this observer chooses what to do. So don't give your subpersonalities the power to run your life as they please.

Teach your inner critic how to speak to you. Help it develop a more encouraging tone.

The next time your inner critic tells you or gives you instructions to do something, ask it to make a suggestion instead. As I have already mentioned, encourage your inner critic to use the word "could" rather than "should," "need to," and "you must." These words give specific directions that will make you feel guilty for not obliging or powerless for obliging. Again, stress to your inner critic that you are more likely to listen if the criticism is guiding and inspiring, rather than demanding and nagging.

Suggestion not only changes the tone of the inner critic, it reminds the inner critic that it is not in control. It can't force or threaten you into doing anything. You have the freedom to choose what is best for you.

3. Let your inner critic know you don't need its protection.

Your inner critic attacks your flaws and imperfections because it thinks this will help you. It wants to protect you from feeling certain emotions such as shame or experiencing certain situations such as failure. To get your inner critic to stop attacking what it perceives to be your flaws and be more compassionate, you need to relay the following messages.

First, let your inner critic know that you are already aware of your imperfections. There is no value in repeating the criticism. Ask your inner critic to stop bringing up the past, too. You have heard it many times before and you have already gotten it.

Second, let your inner critic know that there's nothing

wrong with being imperfect or making mistakes. It's okay to feel shame and to fail. Let it know you can handle these emotions and you accept them completely. You know how to deal with them and release them when they arise.

Lastly, let your inner critic know that criticism doesn't motivate or help you anymore: *Perhaps scolding was what I needed from my parents when I was young to help me navigate the adult world. But now that I am an adult, I understand what is needed to survive. I can decide what's right for me without criticism. I can learn from my own mistakes now. Thank you for your assistance in the past, but there is no need to protect me anymore.*

The reason your inner critic is still with you is that you still need its protection.

Of course, for the above to work, we have to first show our inner critic that we can do it. Just like our over-protective parents, if we want them to stop nagging us, we need to prove that we can take good care of ourselves. Then they will trust and have faith in us. If we welcome all of our emotions and don't resist them, there will be no need for our inner critics to exist. There will be no payoff and they will eventually go away or take a backseat.

Chapter 9

Step #5: Make It a Habit

> *"Peace is a daily, a weekly, a monthly process, gradually changing opinions, slowly eroding old barriers, quietly building new structures."*
>
> — JOHN F. KENNEDY

One day, I noticed something miraculous had happened to me. I accidentally dropped a file on the floor and there was no noise in my head.

Usually, when I dropped my files and the papers were scattered across the floor, the inner critic would tell me off: *How could you be so clumsy and careless? You should have been more careful. Now, you will have to waste your time picking up your papers. Don't you know you're in a hurry?* If not, I would just let out a big sigh or be irritated with my own clumsiness. But that day, there was absolutely no inner critical reaction.

- The file dropped. Fact.
- The paper was scattered on the floor. Fact.
- I picked up the pieces of paper, one by one, and put them back into the file. Action.

I observed what had happened and simply took action. There was no judgment. I was so amazed by how quiet my mind was that I had a mini-celebration. To others, this might not seem like a great deal, but these little changes can show us that we have grown and our effort has paid off. It also reminds us that we can be peaceful at any time and perform the appropriate actions without those chatty voices in our heads.

The objective of this book is not to provide you with a one-off solution that can remove all your self-criticism for good. You have been learning to be self-critical for so long, and it's not easy to change a habit overnight. Even if you manage to stop the negative thoughts from intruding into your mind, it doesn't mean that your mind will get any quieter.

The mind's function is to solve problems and generate thoughts. It can't become peaceful on its own.

The more drama there is, the more problems the mind can solve and the more things it can think about. If there is no problem, your mind will create one to keep itself alive. You need to train your mind to slow down and focus. Whenever your mind strays, gently guide it back to the right path. Only through repetition will the mind learn there is no need to judge all the time.

The mind can be calmer and quieter with practice. Rather than fixing or changing it with force, it's better to devise a plan to deal with it and make the plan a part of your habits. In this way, even if your mind becomes rowdy again, you will know how to handle it and be ready to do so.

How to Devise Your Own Plan

The last step of the Disbelief Process is to make it a habit. In the previous step, you identified the message given by the inner critic and the message has done its job. Now, you can plan your behavior ahead of time and make it a habit.

Planning our behavior or reaction ahead of time intentionally is called the "Implementation Intention," or the "if-then" plan. It was developed and introduced by psychologist Peter Gollwitzer. If you only figure out what to do after you have a critical thought, you are too late. Your mind will have already made you perform in the usual manner.

Implementation Intention allows you to capture your desired behavior beforehand, so when you have a critical thought you know exactly what to do. The structure is as follows:

If (this situation happens),
then I'll perform (this behavior).

For example, when you have a negative thought, stop what you are doing and be aware of the thought. Of course, it's impossible to create the desired behavior for every situation and prepare for all of the situations that might occur in the future. But this book has provided you with a general framework about how to act with regard to your critical thoughts.

Apart from applying the steps in this book, you can add and customize your own steps and make them a part of your plan. Some critical thoughts might need special treatment, and you can come up with an enhanced version of the plan for these thoughts using the information you have collected in the first four steps.

The plan is dynamic. Whenever you receive new information, you can integrate it into your routine and change your plan anytime you want to make it better and keep it updated. You can also test out different methods and see which one suits you the most. Here are three suggestions to help you devise your own plan:

1. Use self-criticism triggers as starting points.

In Chapter 5, I shared four ways in which you can become aware of your thoughts. In Chapter 7, I shared how you can find your self-criticism triggers. Once you know what these triggers are, you can easily use them as starting points.

For example, if you know that making mistakes triggers your inner critic, let it be the trigger for your disbelief routine, too. Whenever you make a mistake, pay attention to your thoughts immediately and begin step #1. By doing this, you can replace your normal reactive behaviors with a new set of habits. Instead of wandering off unconsciously into the comfort of entertainment and food or ruminating on the problem, you can remain alert and catch yourself before you react automatically.

Your cues might be associated with people and location, too. So before you meet people or go to the places that trigger self-criticism, remind yourself to stay alert and be prepared to distance yourself from any thoughts that might arise.

2. Prepare an action to comfort yourself.

Your suffering doesn't have to be painful. It can be used as a trigger to become more compassionate towards yourself. After you have disbelieved your self-criticisms your body might still react to criticism as though it is true. What you can do, other than noticing these reactions, is to prepare another action to comfort the part of you that is being reactive. Sometimes, this might be your inner child or victim subpersonality that feels upset. At times, it could be one of your subpersonalities that is angry and defending its beliefs.

Instead of suppressing these emotions or ignoring their existence, attend to them immediately. Remember, there is a little child inside of you that still feels hurt. Instead of suffering with him or her, be the elder brother or sister for that part of you. Soothe your subpersonalities, care for them, and let them return to their calm states before they snowball into something uncontrollable and strike you when you least expect it.

I prefer to use physical touch because it helps shift my attention from thinking to something tangible. It gets me out of my mental loop. For example, whenever I feel left out or unloved, I'll stroke my left thumb to remind my inner child that I love him. It helps reduce the emotional pain and makes me feel loved.

It takes observation and some trial and error to find the best spot for each type of criticism. This is why noticing your reaction in step #3 is so important. It tells you which part of your body reacts to your negative thoughts. Previously, in Chapter 7, I mentioned that the left-side of my head gets reactive when I overthink. Now, if my mind gets too chatty, I instantly touch the left-side of my head and say, "Ok, I hear you. I get what you are trying to convey. But it's time to stop now. Let's continue another day." This approach helps my mind to become silent. It works like a charm and I use it often when my mind is overly active and I can't sleep.

3. Incorporate what you have learned into your life.

After you have identified the message in step #4, you can

create a new routine to work on the problems you have discovered and improve your life on a regular basis.

For example, if your inner critic often criticized you for being late and you know that timeliness is something you can improve on, then perhaps you can plan in advance when to leave home at the beginning of each day, or you can add a buffer of 15 minutes each time you leave to go somewhere. Making this a daily habit will reduce the need for your inner critic to nag at you.

In my case, my inner critic wasn't happy that I seldom exercise and I wasn't getting my reading done at night. Instead of giving my inner critic the chance to punish me, I started waking up earlier to do my exercise and reading before I start my day proper. By doing this, the inner critic stopped asking me why I didn't do what it had suggested.

Of course, you don't have to do or agree with everything your inner critic tells you. But if you know it's appropriate and you don't do it, then you have not truly listened to the message. It's as though you are listening for the sake of getting the inner critic off your back and you don't really care what the inner critic has to tell you. Listening is only part of the work; the other part is to take action. When you do what you are told, you respect the insights you have received.

Persist Even If You Have Failed

Dr. Wayne Dyer says in his book, *Staying the Path*, "If you slip, it does not mean you are less valuable. It means you have something to learn from slipping." Forming the disbelief habit is the same as any habit formation. Not only do you need a good strategy, it also takes time to get used to your new habit.

Here are some tips that can keep you going and make forming new habits easier.

1. Use reminders.

Don't feel ashamed or dismiss the importance of using reminders. Whether you are just starting out or you have been practicing a habit for a long time, it helps to have reminders. Having a reminder isn't a sign that you are not doing well. Even the Buddhist monks use a mindfulness bell to awaken them from forgetfulness; it's part of their training and practice. Furthermore, forgetting and remembering are both integral parts of the learning process. You can't live without either of them.

I like to document my habit, step by step, on a little piece of paper so I can carry it anywhere I go and refer to it when I forget the next step. You can also paste post-it notes around your house to remind you to be mindful. If you are new to developing a habit, writing down the steps will prevent you from forgetting what to do next.

As mentioned before, you can also attach your new habit to your self-criticism triggers. It will remind you to start your disbelief habit. Another way to do this is to attach it to your daily habits. There are certain actions that we perform daily without fail, such as brushing our teeth or eating our dinner. Doing new habits right after these regular habits will reduce the chances of forgetting to also perform our mindfulness habits.

2. Break the steps into smaller, action steps.

The steps in this book are broad because it helps me get the message across. But you can break it down further into smaller, action steps so that when you read your documented steps, you will know exactly what to do next. For example, when you become aware of your negative thoughts, you can add a sub-step, which is to look at your documented steps. When you disbelieve your thoughts, you can include a step to ask yourself whether the thought is true or not.

Breaking the steps down provides clarity, and you are

more likely to perform the steps because they have become more specific and easier to do. Anyone can look at their documented steps or ask themselves a question; it doesn't take much effort. But if you just tell them to disbelieve their thoughts, they might not know where to start or how to do it.

At the end of this book, you will find a summary of the steps and their sub-steps. You can use it as a reference or starting point to build your own plan.

3. Allow imperfections.

You might find yourself free of negative self-talk for a while, and then one day you realize you are beating yourself up and reacting unconsciously to it again. Realize that this is normal. You don't have to strive for perfection.

Most of us will fluctuate between our new and old habits. We perform our new habits for three straight days and then on the fourth day, we might totally forget about it and revert back to our old habits. Awareness is always there, but we might not recognize it all the time. There will be times when we forget.

Instead of beating yourself up for failing, accept your mistakes and move on. Developing a new habit is not about how many times you did something or how many times you missed it. Habit is a never-ending process that requires you to continue executing something perpetually, despite your previous performance. So take it slow and don't get discouraged by your progress; you are not trying to reach a destination.

Furthermore, change takes time. How long have you been talking negatively to yourself? 5 years? 10 years? 20 years? Don't give up if you have only tried it to change this habit for a week or a month.

4. Celebrate your success.

Most people are aware of when they fail, but they aren't as aware when they succeed. The mind loves spotting problems and when they find them we are easily drawn into the drama. But when there isn't any problem, we tend not to pay attention. When was the last time you noticed your mind was quiet?

Doubting our thoughts and being mindful is actually natural to us. When I was at the river contemplating whether to jump in, I suddenly doubted my suicidal thoughts and woke up from my misery. It just happened spontaneously. I wasn't even thinking about being mindful.

Instead of being mindful by chance, when we include it in our routines, we are making mindfulness intentional.

When you recognize these rare moments of mindfulness (those that happened by chance), celebrate and pay attention to the peace inside of you. Your mind will remember this moment, and all the feelings and sensations, and store it inside your brain for future reference.

5. Reiterate your plan regularly.

There are two purposes in reiterating your plan regularly. One is to keep it fresh and the other is to improve it.

When you keep doing your routine, it might become stale and lose its effectiveness. Sometimes, you need to mix it up a little. The broad steps are most likely going to remain the same, but you can change the sub-steps. Let's say you use the alarm clock to help you become aware of your thoughts. It works for a period of time. But after a while, you start to ignore the alarm because you are too busy with what you are doing. If this is the case, then it's time to change your plan. When you get too used to ignoring your habit, you need something new to reboot it.

Perhaps you can change the alarm to a mindfulness bell instead. Maybe you can install an alarm in your computer desktop to prompt you instead of your mobile phone, or you can change the intervals between the alarm rings, making it longer so you have more time to focus on your work. You might even want to do away with using an alarm and use another way to remind yourself, or just have one review at the end of the day.

I usually change my habit every four months. You don't have to make major changes in your routine; just add what's working and subtract the steps that are working as well. Your habits will change to some degree as you grow.

Final Words

Self-criticism is a habit that can be changed by becoming aware of your reactions. Even though you have no control over all of your thoughts, you have the freedom of choice to believe them or not.

Making an enemy with your mind doesn't help. Instead of fighting your inner critic, be friendly towards it and show compassion. Know that its function is to make a story out of the information that is given. All you need to do is distance your true self from your mind and create a space between you and the mind.

Your unhealthy, habitual ways of thinking are the

result of past conditioning, and they have become a part of your protective mechanism. It's not easy to change this system overnight. Be patient. Slowly and gently guide your mind back to peace. When it resists your guidance, don't push it. When you fail to lead it back to peace, forgive yourself. Every single day, you are given an opportunity to choose. Even if you don't get it right today, tomorrow you will get to choose again.

On the next page, you will find a summary of the Disbelief Process.

I wish you peace and harmony. Good luck!

Summary of the Disbelief Process

Step #1: Be Aware of Your Thoughts

- Use an alarm to check your thoughts regularly.
- Set a clear intention and single-task.
- Listen and journal your thoughts.
- Review your day every evening.

Step #2: Disbelieve All Thoughts

- Listen but maintain a space between your thoughts and your true self.
- Ask yourself, "Is this thought true?"
- Take note that all of the adjectives you use on yourself are a judgment or an opinion; they are not the truth.
- Be aware of words that exaggerate the situation, such as "I should have," "I am always," and "Everyone."

Step #3: Notice Your Reactions

- Anchor to something tangible, such as your breath.
- Pay attention to how your body feels without

describing the sensations in words, at first.

- Write down your reactions after the physical sensations have subsided.
- Identify the self-criticism if you haven't done so in step #1.
- Gather the cues that trigger your self-criticism.

Step #4: Identify the Message

- Respect your inner critic and know it is just doing its job.
- Figure out what the inner critic is trying to protect you from.
- Ask yourself, "Does my past have anything to do with my self-criticism?"
- Focus on the area needing improvement by asking your inner critic to use the words "I could have" instead of "I should have."

Step #5: Make It a Habit

- Devise your own disbelief process using this summary as a starting point.
- Break down the steps and document them on a piece of paper that you can carry with you.

- Set up reminders in your house; for example, put up Post-It notes.
- Attach your disbelief habit to your current habits, if possible.
- Allow imperfections and celebrate your success.
- Revise your plan every four months with the new information you have gained.

Did You Like *The Disbelief Habit*?

Thank you for purchasing my book and spending the time to read it.

Before you go, I'd like to ask you for a small favor. Could you please take a couple of minutes to leave a review for this book on Amazon?

Your feedback will not only help me grow as an author; it will also help those readers who need to hear the message in this book. So, thank you!

Please leave a review at www.nerdycreator.com/the-disbelief-habit.

Recommended Reading

The Fifth Agreement: A Practical Guide to Self-Mastery by Don Miguel Ruiz, Don Jose Ruiz and Janet Mills; 2011; Amber-Allen Publishing, San Rafael, California.

Thinking, Fast and Slow by Daniel Kahneman; 2011; Farrar, Straus and Giroux, New York, New York.

The Art of Thinking Clearly by Rolf Dobelli; 2014; Harper Collins Publishers, New York, New York.

The Power of Habit: Why We Do What We Do in Life and Business by Charles Duhigg; 2012; Random House, New York, New York.

Freedom from Your Inner Critic: A Self-Therapy Approach by Jay Earley PhD and Bonnie Weiss; 2013; Sounds True, Boulder, Colorado.

To read other books on inner critic and negative thinking, visit this URL: http://nerdycreator.com/bookclub/books-to-help-with-negative-thinking/

Notes and References

#Thedress: 'It's been quite stressful having to deal with it ... we had a falling-out' by Leo Benedictus; Decemeber 22, 2015; The Guardian.
https://www.theguardian.com/fashion/2015/dec/22/the-dress-internet-divided-cecilia-bleasdale-black-blue-white-gold

What Colors Are This Dress? by Cates Holderness; February 27, 2015; Buzzfeed.
https://www.buzzfeed.com/catesish/help-am-i-going-insane-its-definitely-blue

#TheDress by Ellen DeGeneres; March 30, 2015; The Ellen Show.
https://www.youtube.com/watch?v=Vu2YZMb4Xb8

What Color Is This Dress? by Mitchell Moffit and Greg Brown; February 27, 2015; AsapSCIENCE.
https://www.youtube.com/watch?v=AskAQwOBvhc

Dove's 'One Beautiful Thought' Shows What It Would Sound Like If Your Inner Critic Spoke Out Loud by Brittany Goldfield Rodrigues; March 30, 2015; Huffington Post.

https://www.huffingtonpost.com/2015/03/30/dove-one-beautiful-thought-campaign_n_6964000.html

Here are more books by Yong Kang:

Empty Your Cup: Why We Have Low Self-Esteem and How Mindfulness Can Help

The Emotional Gift: Memoir of a Highly Sensitive Person Who Overcame Depression

Fearless Passion: Find the Courage to Do What You Love

To see the latest books by the author, please go to www.nerdycreator.com/books.

